Mark Collings has written for leading magazines and newspapers, including *Esquire*, the *Daily Express*, the *Observer* and *Jack*, since 1994.

A VERY BRITISH COOP

Mark Collings had rated pigeons the lowest of the bird family until he met Les Green, head of the UK top pigeon-racing team — known as the 'Salford Mafia' . . . Les, a sharp-tongued ex-gang member, is the author's guide through the weird and wonderful world of British pigeon racing. Pigeons are big business: there are 60,000 pigeon racers in the UK, and rivalry can provoke arson attacks on lofts. *A Very British Coop* is the story of a journey taken from a pigeon loft in Oldham to a shot at the ultimate prize — The Sun City Million Dollar Classic.

MARK COLLINGS

A VERY BRITISH COOP

Pigeon Racing
From Blackpool to Sun City

Complete and Unabridged

ULVERSCROFT
Leicester

First published in Great Britain in 2007 by
Macmillan
an imprint of
Pan Macmillan Limited
London

First Large Print Edition
published 2008
by arrangement with
Pan Macmillan Limited
London

Lyrics from 'Wind Beneath My Wings' reproduced
with the kind permission of Larry Henley.

British Library CIP Data

Collings, Mark
    A very British coop: pigeon racing from Blackpool to
    Sun City.—Large print ed.—
    Ulverscroft large print series: non-fiction
    1. Green, Les 2. Pigeon racing—Great Britain
    3. Large type books
    I. Title
    636.5'96'0941

    ISBN 978-1-84782-437-0

Published by
F. A. Thorpe (Publishing)
Anstey, Leicestershire

Set by Words & Graphics Ltd.
Anstey, Leicestershire
Printed and bound in Great Britain by
T. J. International Ltd., Padstow, Cornwall

This book is printed on acid-free paper

*For Mum and Dad
and in memory of John Green*

Acknowledgements

This book couldn't have been written without the loyal support of my mother and father, my brothers Austin and Jonathan, my sister Beverley and nieces Hope and Milly. It would also have been incredibly difficult to sit at the typer and get this book started and finished without my girlfriend Joanne O'Connor, my agent David Luxton and my publisher at Macmillan, Richard Milner. All of the above gave me nothing but good sense and encouragement at the right time and all were astute enough to know when the moment was correct to administer a gentle nudge or a kick up the arse.

I would also like to thank the pigeon racing fraternity for all their help and generosity while I was researching and writing this book, and also for the many laughs and the mad and mostly truthful stories that kept me warmed and entertained in the numerous lofts and bars up and down the country. Thanks pigeon men and women of Britain and the world! With extra special salutations to the one and only Les Green and his wife Ruth, Tess Green, Ray Lunt, Gary Wall, Paul

Galley, Pat (for the black pudding and cheese offers), Bobby Rimmer, Andy Jiggins, Stuart Elvin, Paul Smith, Zandy Meyer, Michael Shepherd, Tony Cowan, Peter Bryant, Gerard Koopman, Jimmy Richards, Joe Gomes, Laurence Lauder, Ron MacFayden, Sun International for helping out with the trip to Sun City, Frank, Colin and the late great Moonie.

A final doffing of the cap goes to all the friends and acquaintances whose lives were sometimes invaded with tales of pigeon derring do. In no particular order: ta very much to Kevin Mitchell, Mark Bowes, Emmanuel Ohajah, Shane Starling, Mark Chambers, Ian Walker, Grant Skehill, Phil Hayess, Kurt Haslam, Jimmy Muffin and, the two men who could drive a brother of the sacred order to distraction, the Tommy Dunns, both Sr and Jr, and all their clan.

Contents

Prologue

Colin

So where did it all begin, my pigeon odyssey? With tragedy and comedy and a kid called Colin.

Every school has its Colin — the awkward kid who is a lightning conductor for the bullies. It just so happened our Colin was called Colin.

Back in the early 1980s, our Colin had a small pigeon loft and with the help of his granddad Frank flew around thirty grey checker pigeons (so called because of the dark check markings on the wings) every weekend in the summer months, with varying degrees of success.

He was the typical hard luck case, unfairly burdened with a raft of problems before he could lace his own monkey boots. He was fatherless and clumsy and had the shape and complexion of a Bernard Matthews butterball turkey. Hassle and trouble of the juvenile kind seemed to attach themselves to Colin and follow him like sheets of wet toilet paper on the sole of his shoe.

At school Colin seemed always to be under some kind of attack: if he wasn't being shouted at for his all-round doziness, he was dodging a teacher's board rubber or the foot of some young toerag. Not surprisingly he would often bunk off school and hang around the old disused railway embankment looking for useful scraps to add to his pigeon loft, or finding frogs and newts and any small living thing that he could grab hold of and drop into an old paint tin and then take back home to store, nurture or whatever on earth he did with them.

Colin seemed happier around animals and birds and anything else that didn't want to shove his head down a toilet or kick him up the arse. It kept him sane until he learned the basic lessons of survival and until he developed a penchant for telling lies to garner favours and attention of the more palatable kind with the rougher kids at school.

Colin told lies to gain a bit of breathing space. He was desperate. You can only take so much bag carrying and knuckle rapping before you start to unravel. Amongst other things he told whoever would listen that his mother worked at a cigarette factory (he didn't specify which one). This helped for a while, but it was a double-edged sword as the hard cases would demand cigs and Colin would have to lift them from his mum's purse. Colin also proclaimed loudly — and most impressively of all — that he was related to a popular wrestler of the day known as 'deaf and dumb' — Alan Kilby.

For anybody who doesn't remember, Alan Kilby was a regular on the Saturday afternoon wrestling on ITV hosted by Kent Walton, and due to his disabilities was something of an outsider. Although unlike Colin he was a popular outsider. Clad in his tight leotard, the grapple fans loved Alan for the ineffable determination he showed in over-coming his clearly stated disabilities, as well as his formidable mastery of the forearm smash.

Colin's claim was intended for those with designs on raiding his pockets of small change and cigs but there was also maybe a more subtle message that he too, like the wrestler, had hidden depths. Sadly, however, it didn't wash and he was condemned to several terms of lifting money as well as cigarettes from his mum's purse to keep the groin stompers from subjecting him to their own version of the forearm smash.

In his spare time Colin's small yellow pigeon loft — (brightly coloured to attract the birds) — at the back of his house was his passion and personal retreat. He would tend to his pigeons after school and along with his granddad would carefully feed and train them each evening (or during the day if he was bunking off and his mother wasn't around). I saw the thirty or so birds swirl up into the sky once or twice on the way back from school, when Colin was training them for the Saturday race, and there was a simple and unpretentious grace to the way they stuck together in a tight bunch before they flew off into the distance. At least that's the way I remember it now — at the time I hardly gave them a second thought. But Colin's loft, his retreat, didn't last. Things like that rarely did in Radcliffe.

Radcliffe is a rank brew of the urban and the rural. Known to locals as 'dogshit valley', it's a mixture of farms, fields and council estates. For some — like Colin — who needed to escape, the pull of nature was the strongest but it was those who preferred the concrete to the fields, the training shoes to the wellies, who ruled the roost in the valley of the dog-turds. Colin's loft was a regular target for snipers wearing Farah slacks and carrying air rifles. You had to fit in or you took your chances and, because Colin stuck out like a canary in a pigeon coop, he awoke one morning — despite many efforts to repel the barbarians — to find the loft had been raided and the pigeon holes were empty.

The mystery of the missing pigeons became quite a story for a week or two after that — like a small-scale Shergar or Lord Lucan. Who had raided Colin's loft and why? Was it a jealous rival or just a spiteful nutter? The local paper deemed it worthy of half a page and a small picture of a very solemn Colin pointing to an empty pigeon loft. It was all fairly tragic. Poor Colin was such an enthusiast that pigeon racing was the one thing he didn't have to lie about. But despite the press and public awareness of the missing contents of Col's coop the birds were never found and Colin had to start from scratch before he could fly pigeons again. Which was tough. Pigeon racing, even then, wasn't cheap if you wanted to be competitive, and Colin had to sell his bike and various other knick-knacks to help rebuild the loft in a safer place.

The mystery remained until several years after we had left school when a local bruiser, giddy through a haze of strong lager, admitted he had stolen the pigeons due to a promise of an exclusive audience with 'deaf and dumb' Alan Kilby which never came to pass, and which he had paid a tenner for. Nothing could justify the dastardly deed but

Colin's weakness for telling porkies had backfired horribly. The loft raider sold the pigeons to a local Chinese chip shop for £2 each and then treated himself to an Adidas tracksuit and several nights on the cider.

The final agonizing twist was that Colin regularly ate at the chippy so there was a good chance he may have been reunited with at least one of his beloved pigeons at some point after the disappearance. Tragedy and comedy. That's how it started and over twenty years later that's how it began again.

1

Pigeon men are born to it

'Remember that you are a human being with a soul and the divine gift of articulate speech: that your native language is the language of Shakespeare and Milton and The Bible; and don't sit there crooning like a bilious pigeon.'

George Bernard Shaw, *Pygmalion*

'Les, I'm lost,' I said.

'Fuckin' hell. You're not much cop, are you? Hurry up you daft bastard you're late.' Les's Salford accent was as stodgy as a steak pudding but I sensed a friendly tone beneath the volley of expletives.

'It's the house with the pigeons on the gate,' he said, and then he was gone.

I was standing outside a newsagent's next to a sandwich board with the headline 'PAKISTANI FAMILY TRY TO TAKE CORPSE ON PLANE AS HAND LUGGAGE'. Les lived in Irlam. Irlam was in Salford. It was a small town about eight or nine miles outside Manchester, a fight-outside-the-chippy sort

7

of town, but slightly better — certainly no worse — than any other place in Salford.

I followed Les's instructions. I walked down a road lined with council bungalows, with twitching net curtains, and then past a row of shops with a Booze Buster off licence, Eurotan solarium and a pet shop with the bold message in the window that 'Kittens and Maggots are back in stock!' I walked down Silver Street and Woodbine Terrace and stumbled on the neat semi with the pigeon engravings on the gate where Les and his small family resided.

'You're a useless fucker aren't ye?' said Les. He was waiting at the gate wearing a blue loft overall, liberally covered in pigeon guano. Underneath the loft coat was a T-shirt and three-quarter-length shorts which revealed a pair of pale calves that had the chunky muscularity of a pub league footballer. Les extended a thick-fingered hand. 'How are ya, mate?'

★ ★ ★

Les was going to be my guide through pigeon racing, and lord knows I needed one because my knowledge of the pigeon, in any shape or form, was distinctly lacking. In fact, if pressed, I couldn't spot a racing bird from a street pecker squatting in Nelson's hat. Like most people, if I gave them a second thought — which was rare — I had all of them lumped in together, the racing birds and the common street pigeon, or the 'feral' pigeon as it's called by those in the know. They were all the same to me; cloud vermin, winged scruffs, flying rats and any other unpleasant moniker you could conjure to describe the *Columba livia*. I certainly would not have associated the creatures who would keep me up at night scratching in the guttering with the sleek, feathered dynamos that are known in the game as 'athletes of the sky'.

So how did I find Les Green, and why? Les Green, the 'guv'nor' of the north-west pigeon racing scene and the fast-talking front man of the 'Salford Pigeon Mafia'. And how did I end up spending a year of my life in and around the pigeon lofts of Great Britain? Like most things it happened by accident. Pure chance and a little bit of desperation thrown in. I was having a bad time. My long-term relationship had broken down, I had debts and rent to pay and I hadn't had a decent story idea for weeks.

I'd given up my job to make it as a full-time writer but the work had dried up and it was getting to the point were I would be forced to temp in some dreary office if something didn't happen soon. The turgid symphony of inane banter and frustration wafting over those grey synthetic carpets that conspired to give you an electric shock every time you left your squeaky chair was still fresh in my mind. A crisis loomed but I tried not to panic.

Self doubt, fear and the landlord began to knock loudly at my door. I lay on the couch most days, channel-hopping through the morass of cable TV channels, distracted and numbed with the terrible thought that maybe I'd made the wrong decision by turning my back on the steady job. The terror-induced inertia went on for weeks until my remote control landed on a rerun of *Bullseye* on UK Gold.

'I hear you've got an interesting story, Rod?' said the 1987 version of Jim Bowen to a contestant who was wearing a dark suit and tie and was sporting a thin neatly trimmed moustache.

'Yes, I race pigeons, Jim,' said Rod.

For some reason — as enigmatic and mysterious as the homing instinct of the pigeon itself — I shifted my attention from the tin of biscuits on my lap to the rerun of the darts quiz show and listened to Rod with some degree of interest.

Rod was from Barrow-in-Furness and his

hair was thinning, dyed a blue/black colour and greased back off his forehead. He looked a bit like an ageing Gomez from the Addams Family. He didn't have long to say his piece but he made the most of it. I sat transfixed while munching on a pink wafer from the family assortment.

Rod told Jim that he'd had several champions of the feathered variety and had recently encountered some trouble with vandals at the loft which had culminated in several missing birds and a desire for a civil prosecution. Rod looked serious for a moment but Jim lightened the mood with a joke and Rod — cheered by the gag — finished off by telling Jim that winning a pigeon race was better than sex with his wife. Although he didn't say that, he said: 'a bit of you-know-what with the wife'.

Rod, Jim and the audience of pensioners laughed — about the sex, not the vandalism and the missing birds. 'Great. What a lovely story and a lovely man. Give him a round of applause,' said Jim. And Rod and his partner went on to win £75 and a tumble dryer.

I wouldn't exactly call it an epiphany but it was as near as I was going to get sitting on the couch watching daytime TV. Pigeon racing? I wasn't sure why but I liked it. It wasn't going to dent the armour of the debt-filled juggernaut that was thundering towards me but I had a good feeling about it. The next day I was on the phone to a magazine editor who threw me occasional scraps.

'Pigeon racing?' There was a pause at the other end before the weary voice of the editor said, 'Sounds all right.'

I thought the next logical step was to find Colin or the bloke from *Bullseye* but I decided that it was more realistic to pursue Colin. The darts quiz show hadn't been on our screens for over fifteen years and Rod was knocking on a bit when it had originally aired. I rang a couple of friends from school to see if they could throw any light on Colin's whereabouts but they had no idea. I subscribed to Friends Reunited but again no luck. Colin had seemingly flown the coop. But I didn't want to give up on the story. I knew there was something in it.

It seemed to me that pigeon racing as a sport — if it could be classified a sport — was, like Colin, a rank outsider and it had the musty cloak of British eccentricity draped over it. Maybe that was the reason for its 'rank outsider' status. It was antiquated, and totally at odds with the carefully preened and coiffeured sports that dominated the early part of the twenty-first century, and as attractive to the iPod generation as a ferret down the trouser leg or a plate of tripe. But I liked that. One man in his loft against the world — or if not the world then at least the bloke down the street. The smell of creosote and bird seed in the nostrils. There was a simple nobility to it, a sense of duty and purpose imbued with the quixotic spirit. A potent mixture of defiance, skill and stupidity. What drove a man or a woman to devote such a great amount of time and effort to such an unpopular creature? I really wanted to know. And I was getting a bit closer to finding out.

'Pigeon men are born to it. It's an obsession that takes over everything. It's hard to explain,' said Frank as he drained what was left of his pint of bitter. 'When you watch those birds appear on race day and they begin their descent into the loft it's like nothing you've ever seen or experienced. It's fuckin' poetic,' he said, and then he sat back and stared sagely at his now empty glass.

Frank was Colin's granddad. I'd tracked him down to a pub within spitting distance of where they used to keep their first loft. Frank hadn't gone far. I should have known.

Frank was in his late seventies now but he was still putting the pints of bitter away with reassuring efficiency. He had that unshake-able docker's thirst. Frank had worked on the

Salford docks most of his life — unloading large bags of grain and meat from Canada and various other places on number nine dock until the late seventies — and he'd seen a thing or two. The only problem was he had been drinking when he'd seen most of it, and it was touch and go if he remembered much; and if he did was any of it true?

'Get one in will ye, our kid?' he said, lifting up the empty glass.

Before I tracked him down I was told to watch out for a well-thumbed Polaroid of a blurred hand with a ring on the finger which Frank would often pull from the coat pocket of his old blazer. 'That was me and Sinatra,' he would say, pointing at the hand in the photo. 'Great mates, me and Ol' Blue Eyes.' Frank Christian Andersen, as he was known to some locals who drank in the same pubs, or simply 'bullshitter Frank' to the less discerning and well-read clientèle.

As well as his love of pigeons, Colin's youthful diversions from the truth were more than likely inherited from his granddad. Some lucky souls get money or a house — Colin got a loft full of pigeons and lessons in the art of bullshitting. Them's the breaks.

I placed Frank's pint on the table and as I sat down I saw him reach into his pocket. I thought he was either going to give me money for the drink or reveal the picture of the hand, so I quickly asked for his grandson's whereabouts. Frank sucked down a good portion of the pint and then said:

'Budapest.'

'Budapest? On holiday?'

'No. He married a girl from over there. They run a guest house. A hotel.'

Budapest? Colin? This was getting ridiculous. Did I need the pigeon racing story this bad? I wasn't sure whether to believe old Frank but no matter. As the afternoon unfolded it became obvious that his grandson was no longer around, either that or Frank thought I was some kind of spook and wasn't for giving up a contact number. Probably somewhere in between. I eventually left Frank to his beer and tall tales, feeling a little drunk and deflated.

When I sobered up I realized there could be no room for sentimentality if I wanted the story. If I needed to get the inside track on pigeons I would have to forget about a reunion with Colin for a while. I cleared my head and went a different route. I rang my pal Bobby.

Bobby trained boxers for a living, and flew pigeons in his spare time. He knew people from all avenues, cul de sacs and dead ends of life, and was something of an item himself,

15

having found pugilism and pigeon fancying by way of Strangeways and various other institutions patronized by Her Majesty the Queen. I'd known Bobby for a while and I trusted his instinct for a character, so I rang him and explained my predicament.

'Les Green,' said Bobby without hesitation. 'If you want to talk pigeons Les is the guv'nor . . . The Master,' he enthused.

That was good enough for me. Bobby gave me The Master's number so I made the call and a few days later I was admiring the pigeon engravings on Les Green's gate.

'Just wait there a minute,' Les said before bouncing back into his neat semi and reappearing with a big man with tattoos on each forearm.

'Thanks, Les. Appreciate that,' said the man with tattoos. Les waved him off at the gate then turned to me and pointed at the van driving away.

'See that bloke? He came down five years ago to buy some pigeons. He's from Lanarkshire. He spent a couple of nights in a hotel and paid us to teach him how to buy pigeons and that has made him the best fancier that Scotland has ever seen. That is no word of a lie, they've never seen owt like him in Scotland. He's a fuckin' marvel up there.'

Les Green was in his early forties and bore

16

no resemblance to the widely perceived 'flat cap and whippet' image of the pigeon racer. There was no cloth cap or wiry mutt, just a shaven head, a goatee beard and a well-worn pair of Adidas Samba trainers.

He was more Shaun Ryder than Jack Duckworth, and he had the broad-shouldered build of a nightclub bouncer (which he was for several years). Les was hefty with thick arms and neck, but not the physique of the gym rat. Les's brawn was more of your steak-pudding than the steroid-enhanced variety. He had a labourer's bulk and it was matched with a mouth like the inside of a cement mixer.

There is a long and fine tradition of Mancunians/Salfordians with mouths as filthy as the Irwell but Les was up there with the finest. Apart from Bernard Manning I'd never heard anyone swear with as much gusto as Les Green. Expletives, like his gap-toothed grin, were never far from his lips, and they flew from his mouth with regularity and flair.

'This phone never stops ringin',' said Les, turning off his mobile and stuffing it back into his overalls. 'I get more calls than the fuckin' Samaritans.'

Les's house was a family home: he had three kids, but it was neat and tidy apart from the odd WWF wrestling figure and Bratz doll

17

scattered around the kitchen.

'Nice trophies, Les,' I said, admiring Les's small collection of shiny pigeon trophies.

'Oh, we've got hundreds of 'em. Trophies and rosettes up in the loft. Need an extension to keep 'em all in.'

Les wanted to know if I was a fancier or a 'pigeon man', as he called it. I told him I wasn't. I said that I didn't have the first idea about pigeons but I was intrigued. I was on a fact-finding mission and I wanted to know the secrets of his success and the ways of the pigeon and those who flew them.

'Well, if you want to know about pigeons you've come to the right place,' said Les matter of factly as he placed two cups on the *Snow White* tablecloth.

'I'm not blowing our own trumpet here but we, me and my partners, are the best. We are taking the game to a new level in this country. No one has results like us and that's a fact.'

That afternoon Les showed me a folder of files stuffed with the results from several seasons of racing. He thumbed through each sheet eagerly, stopping to point out each triumph that appeared in black and white. I knew nothing — it may well have been written in Aramaic for all I knew — but it sounded impressive.

'We had the first twelve in that race, the

first eight in that, the first ten in that ... unheard of, these results,' said Les, pointing and flipping over one sheet of numbers after the next.

Les talked with great enthusiasm and in detail about the birds he had reared and flown with enormous success throughout Britain, and sometimes into France, for over ten years. He talked with passion, hardly pausing to draw a breath. He talked at length about past greats like The Prince who won twenty-five first prizes and was the ace bird of the combine seven times, Golden Wonder who was sold for £4,500, and the remarkable Grey Gem who won the area title seventeen times and once flew back to the loft with a broken leg after hitting an electricity pylon.

Les clearly loved his pigeons and held a lifelong ambition for his team to be recognized as the 'Manchester United of pigeon racing'. Les wasn't in the pigeon game to mess around. He had big plans. He had ideas. He wanted the RPRA (Royal Pigeon Racing Association) to ditch the old manual clock timing system and bring in the new ETS (Electronic Timing System), and he wanted football-style leagues set up — with promotion and relegation.

And the plans didn't stop with racing. He wanted to breed new strains of *über* pigeons.

He told me he and his partners often travelled around Europe to pick up any piece of information they could to get an edge on their rivals, buying birds and knowledge from Holland and Belgium and Germany, where pigeon racing was 'like a national sport'.

'The numbers may be declining over here but the quality of the pigeons has risen and there's certainly more money in it than there was. There's big dosh in it now,' said Les as he carefully placed his file of results back in the cupboard. 'There are big-money races all over the world: America, Australia, Taiwan, Cardiff. You name it. And there's the Million Dollar race in Sun City.'

As I got ready to leave Les reached into his pocket and turned his mobile phone back on. As soon as he did it was ringing. More pigeon business. He left the room and came back twenty minutes later with a broad grin.

'Never fuckin' stops. I got a call last night from a guy in the north-east. He says, 'Are you Les Green? Well, listen. My pigeons are flying for an hour and a half and when they get in to the loft they are bouncing all over the place, really healthy, but they're two minutes behind on a Saturday when I'm racing 'em. What's wrong with 'em?' I said, 'How do I know what's fuckin' wrong with 'em? Who d'you think I am, Doctor fuckin' Dolittle?''

I left Les's place impressed. He was clearly a man with a rare talent and one whose life ambition was not only to dominate the pigeon-flying arenas of the north but to help drag the sport into the twenty-first century.

The magazine was also cock-a-hoop with the tale of Les, 'the bird man of Irlam', and the story ran several months later. Things were looking up but shortly after Les appeared on the news-stands the magazine folded. Although the two events weren't connected, I was told. No matter. I was back to square one. Broke, sitting around moping and channel-hopping. I needed a way out. I gave it some thought and then I rang Les again.

'Come down to the loft and I'll show you the birds,' he said. 'You'll be impressed. Marvellous fuckin' things they are.'

2

The Salford Pigeon Mafia

'Pound for pound, *Columba livia* (the pigeon) is one of the smartest, most physically adept creatures in the animal kingdom.'

www.pigeons.com

'Watch out for the dog,' said Les as he opened the steel door and led me into an old factory that was mission control for 'Northern Premier Promotions' — aka Wall, Lunt, Galley and Green, pigeon supremos. 'It'll drag you in and rip your throat out.'

It was late August, raining, and mission control was in an old factory building that used to be a brewery on a small industrial estate in Oldham. It wasn't glamorous (in fact in Les's words it was a 'fucking shithole') but the factory was the base of operations for the partners and their team of around 150 racing birds who resided in an eighty-foot loft that Les, Ray and Gary had built on the factory roof.

'This doesn't look like much in here,' said

Les referring to the debris-filled factory floor, 'but it's like a five star hotel in that pigeon loft. You just wait and see,' he said, and then he slammed the door shut. 'Just walk up to the end there but mind that fuckin' dog.'

As well as the pigeons the factory was home to another creature of the non-human variety. A dog. And not just any old dog but a salivating and savage German Shepherd guard dog that was so lacking in charm Les hadn't bothered to name it. He just referred to it as 'that fuckin' dog'.

I walked through the musty ground floor, stepping over the odd dead rat, rusty can and piece of rotting timber, towards a small wooden staircase. 'If you want to keep your leg, make sure you keep left when you get to the bottom of those stairs,' said Les.

I wanted to keep my leg. Both legs in fact. So I followed Les's advice as I carefully stepped onto the narrow wooden staircase leading up to the loft. The dog's abode was in a dark corner next to the staircase in a makeshift wooden pen that looked like it would sag and fall over with one firm push. I discovered this as I placed my foot on the second step of the stairs and the pen wobbled, and I was suddenly greeted by the snapping jaws of the vicious hound.

'STAND TO THE LEFT OR IT'LL 'AVE

YOUR FUCKIN' LEG OFF!' Les shouted as the dog leapt and tried to drag me into its lair. I climbed the stairs with my back pinned to the wall as the beast lunged for any piece of me it could get its yellow gnashing teeth on. Les laughed loudly at the bottom of the staircase as I finally reached the safety of the roof, sweating and shaking and relieved to feel the Oldham wind and drizzle on my face.

'Met the dog 'ave you?' On the roof I was greeted by one of Les's partners, Ray Lunt. 'Can't be too careful. People 'ave had lofts burnt down in this business you know,' said Ray, laughing. He was small and stocky, wearing a stained blue fleece and a scruffy grey woollen hat. To settle myself I lit up a cigarette. 'Make sure you don't drop the dimps on the floor,' said Ray. 'The pigeons will eat 'em. Come on in. I'll make you a brew.'

He led me into a small wooden cabin that smelt like an old pet shop. Gary Wall, the third member of the team, was sat in a corner rolling a cigarette from a tin of tobacco. He was taller than Ray and he was wearing a flat cap. 'All right?' said Gary quietly as he licked the cigarette paper.

There was a gas stove in the cabin and a sink full of pots and pans, and a TV in the corner. Underneath the TV were three large

24

black plastic bins that I assumed were filled with pigeon feed.

I peered into one of the bins and as I did Les crept into the hut and grabbed my leg. I jumped and everyone laughed apart from me. 'He likes you, that fuckin' dog. I can tell,' said Les.

★ ★ ★

Les was born and raised in Ordsall, a hard Salford town with close geographical and spiritual links to Manchester United. Ordsall is just a short drive from Old Trafford and was once the home of Eddie Coleman — Busby Babe and victim of the Munich air disaster. It was built around the docks and the dye factories that withered in the 1970s and finally croaked in the early 1980s. You needed to be tough to get through a childhood with your faculties and limbs intact, and Les was tough all right. Les was, in his own words, a 'tearaway, a right little bastard' and he would often bunk off school and break into local mills and factories to steal whatever he could, including birds eggs of any kind. That's where the pigeon fancying started — when Les was twelve years old and with a handful of stolen eggs from the Palmolive soap factory.

Les's first pigeon loft was on derelict land near a local church. During the summer holidays he and his pals persuaded the vicar to let them clean up the disused plot in exchange for the vicar's permission to build a pigeon loft on it. The man of the cloth agreed and Les and his mates were in business. 'We robbed all this fencing and wood from the church and fenced the church off and that's how it all started,' said Les, scraping a bit of pigeon crap off his blue overall.

When he wasn't fighting or robbing Les spent most of his time with the pigeons. It gave him space and time to himself that he couldn't find anywhere else and it kept him busy (he liked to be busy). He needed to channel the excess energy that had got him into so many scrapes into something more constructive than cracking heads, and the pigeons helped him. But there was more to it than that. He also enjoyed the responsibility of nurturing a bird from the egg, watching it grow and develop into something other than a scruffy street roamer.

Les got his share of stick for devoting so much time to pigeons but he laughed it off and if anyone got too out of line he would sock them in the jaw. 'Other kids thought I was a bit of a twat back when I was a kid,' said Les, picking up two slices of Warburton's bread and placing them in the toaster. 'Messing about with the pigeons. They thought I was a bit of a crank but what the fuck did they know? My brothers-in-law would see me carrying water for the pigeons and they'd say to Ruth, my wife, 'Look at him. What a dickhead. What the fuck are you going out with him for?' But look at us now.'

★ ★ ★

Thirty years later and they didn't think Les was a crank any longer. He made a healthy living out of his pigeon 'obsession' and he enjoyed his work. He laughed and joked a lot and it was the good pure laugh of a man who couldn't believe his luck; a man whose life could have turned bad but was actually just fine. With Les there seemed a palpable sense of relief that things were OK. In fact better than OK. Les was the lead part in one of the best pigeon racing and breeding forces in the UK, and to him time in the loft didn't seem like work at all.

'He couldn't get enough of the pijins when he was a kid,' said Ray when Les had left the cabin. 'He wanted to know everything. You've got to have pijins in your blood and you could tell that Les had it in his blood even back then.'

Ray and Gary were ten years older than Les and had raced pigeons all their lives. 'We could see that Les had what it took. You could tell he loved it. He would come up to the loft when he was wagging school and mither me to death,' said Ray with a smile. Both Ray and Gary could see that the young Les had the potential to be a big noise in what Ray calls the 'pijin business'.

The dynamic trio joined forces in the early nineties — the threesome became a foursome in 2003 when Les's mate Paul Galley joined the team — and within a couple of years they were dominating the north-west pigeon flying competitions. According to Les nobody had seen anything like it. Pigeon fanciers the length and breadth of Britain were astonished by the 'talent' flying from the lofts of Wall, Lunt and Green. In a short space of time — certainly in terms of pigeon rearing and racing — Nationals were won with minutes to spare and records broken more often than bird shit falls in Trafalgar Square.

However, the meteoric rise to the top of the pigeon racing heap was greeted with mixed reactions from some rivals. Les with his fearsome dedication, together with his shaven head, bouncer's physique and outspoken views on how pigeon racing should be organized, intimidated some of the older racers and tongues began to wag.

'To be honest with you, people began to fuckin' hate us because of who we were,' said Les, lobbing pigeon feed from one hand to the other and looking like he really didn't care if some of his rivals hated him or not. 'Pigeon racing is the only sport where you can start to compete with the best straight away: if you start today, you start against the champions. Like a pub team joining the Premiership. People get jealous and get hurt. Even in golf you start with a handicap, so it's not fair really. It's the only sport like that.' I asked Les whether pigeon racing was actually a sport. 'Well, not exactly, because you don't directly participate. But fuck me, when was the last time you saw a greyhound trainer chasing the rabbit round the track, and greyhound racing is a sport.'

On a cold January night in Blackpool on the eve of the National Pigeon Racing Convention in 2001, a rival spotted Les and his burly pals swaggering through the sticky-carpeted halls of the Savoy hotel and ran for cover. 'Here come the mafia!' he shouted down the smoky halls.

'Cheeky bastard,' said Les. 'I wouldn't mind but this bloke was a right wrong 'un and didn't even know us. It's jealousy. But that's the typical British for yer. They love to knock the winner. In this country they love to back a loser. They loved Frank Bruno, and Eddie the Eagle, the worst fuckin' ski jumper in the world, became a national hero. They love a wanker; he was on every chat show and he was the biggest wanker we've ever had. They love a loser don't they, the English, typical Brits who love to knock a winner. We are at the top of our game, we are the best and everybody knows we are, nobody can dispute that.'

In their eyes Wall, Lunt, Galley and Green were revolutionaries rather than rabble-rousers. Innovators. Like the Hungarian football team who trounced England in 1952, or Sugar Ray Robinson (the great boxer who inspired Muhammad Ali), they applied new methods to their 'sport' that pushed the boundaries of what had been seen before. It was pigeon racing alchemy, gleaned from some of the great pigeon minds of Holland and Belgium and given the Salford spin, and Ray reckoned it ruffled a lot of feathers in the pigeon-racing fraternity.

'They were going to burn us at the stake. We developed a system where we could race females and get great performances from them, and we did the same with young birds too,' said Ray, removing his grey woollen hat and scratching his head.

The system they developed was called the 'darkness' system. And it was so effective rivals thought that Les and his team were feeding the birds steroids or some other illegal substance to enhance the performances. The rivals were so concerned they took to hiding out near Les's loft and spying with binoculars to see if Les was fiddling the times or 'juicing them up'.

'We basically made the youngsters think it was winter when it was summer,' said Ray with a shrug of the shoulders. 'The reason for that is nature tells the pigeon to grow new feathers for when the days are long, and you've got all day to forage for the food. In the winter when times are hard you keep all your feathers and nurture all your energy, so we make these pigeons think it's winter when it's summer.' This meant that the pigeon didn't waste valuable energy growing new feathers, and could use this energy to fly faster.

'On every door there's a shutter and we pull them down when we put the bird in. We just give them eight hours light every day so they think it's winter hours. Doesn't matter about the temperature. We spent a weekend with a guy in Holland who was at it and we paid him to tell us what the crack was. We brought the system back in 1994 and employed it here. They'd never seen anything like it. They couldn't believe it. Well, we couldn't, really. It was unreal and we got a lot of shit for it but I suppose that's the price you pay for being good at something.'

However, it's hard to keep secrets for too long in the pigeon business and the darkness system was quickly uncovered and adopted by other racers who were brassed off with trailing so far behind Les. 'It's about staying one step ahead of your rivals,' said Les. 'Trying to get the edge but it never lasts. That's why you've got to stay on top of it. If you blink someone else has got the edge and you're left eating his feathers.'

Les's loft was split into several sections to separate the youngest pigeons from the oldest, and the cocks from the hens. This, Les told me, was simply to prevent the younger and more immature birds from disturbing the older ones and the 'cocks from shagging the hens'. Nearest to the cabin were the 'babies', who were three months and under, in the middle were the 'young 'uns', who were three to six months old, with the older birds housed in the sections at the end of the loft.

Les slid the dark brown doors to one of the sections open and we stepped inside. The loft was clean apart from the odd pigeon dropping here and there. Les liked to keep it clean so the birds felt happier and more comfortable, so he scrubbed it three or four times a day.

Thirty six-month-old pigeons were sat in their wooden pigeon holes quietly cooing, blinking and pecking on some kind of feed in a small tray. As we entered they hardly flapped a wing or turned a head. Les talked quietly as though he was in a library or a cathedral.

'We call her Madonna,' Les said, pointing to a grey pigeon who was chomping on something or other. ''Cause she swings both ways. Has lesbian tendencies, that one.'

Les picked up a broom and began to sweep the small amount of crap on the floor. The birds still hardly moved. 'They love me, you see, and they are used to me,' said Les by way of an explanation. 'See, in a lot of lofts you wouldn't get them as well behaved as that.'

He picked one of his birds up and cradled it, gently pulling its wings out and stroking them. 'All right, beautiful?' he said to the grey checker pigeon. 'This one's doing well at the moment. Beautiful aren't you, darling?'

'Has it got a name?' I asked.

'No. She hasn't developed a character yet. Sometimes it takes a while for them to do that.'

I stared at the pigeon and it blinked several times. I didn't know if it was beautiful or not. It was cleaner than a street pigeon, the green and red markings on its breast were shiny and I thought it looked quite big for such a young bird. 'That's not big,' said Les dismissively. 'That's average. They're ready to fly at three months.'

He stood for a moment, cradling and stroking the bird in silence. The pigeon seemed quite content with the attention it was receiving. It was remarkably well behaved. Certainly none of Les's pigeons seemed to have the urge to make a rush for the open door and chomp on the soggy burger bun that was sat in the puddle outside, or hover above my head and drop anything on my shoulder. I complimented Les on their impeccable behaviour.

'Well, you know why that is? Because we treat 'em like fuckin' royalty, that's why. They get better fed and looked after than a lot of kids around here.'

Late August was coming up, as was the end of the pigeon racing season, which ran from April to late September. In the first few months of the season the older birds (1–2 years old) raced, and in the latter half of the season the younger birds (aged 3–6 months) were flown competitively. Les and his team had success with all the birds they raced, regardless of age. And they'd had a typically successful season in 2005. They'd had thirty-nine first prizes and topped the federation ten times — a record in Oldham — and won 'Ace bird of the combine' with a pigeon called Blue Wonder.

Wall, Lunt, Galley and Green's club was in Denton, one of twelve clubs in the Oldham Federation, which had approximately forty-two members and 600 racing birds. Pigeon racing in the UK is split into club, federation, amalgamation and combine races. The federation is usually made up of around ten or twenty clubs in a twenty-mile radius. An amalgamation is made up of clubs within a forty-mile radius and the combine is within a sixty- to seventy-mile radius. The national races encompass every club and the whole of the country.

Les placed the bird back in its hole and we walked out of the loft closing the door quietly. 'There's a science to pigeon racing.' Les had swept the burger bun out of the puddle and was staring out over the council estates and mills of Oldham towards the Pennine hills. 'It's not just a matter of cleaning the shit out of the loft once a day.'

The successful pigeon racer needs to be an animal psychologist as well as a vet, Les told me. Pigeons are a twenty-four-hour, seven-day-a-week job. You are always on call and always thinking about them.

'There are nights when I can't sleep because I'm thinking about 'em. They are on my mind all the time. They don't know when it's your kid's birthday or when it's Christmas,' said Les. 'They want feeding and watering no matter what.'

Les needed to basket the birds up and get them ready for a race on Saturday. As he pulled down the baskets from inside the cabin I told him that I was interested in buying a pigeon of my own and racing him.

'It's a big commitment, ya know? It's like caring and providing for another family. You wouldn't believe the dedication it takes. You can buy a McLaren car but it doesn't mean you can drive like Michael Schumacher. Any old Tom, Dick or Harry can't just buy a pigeon and be successful with it.'

I told him I wasn't looking at pigeon racing as a long-term career move.

'It doesn't work like that,' he said as he placed a bird into the basket and closed the lid. 'These pigeons are top quality. It's a serious business. Marriages have broken down because of pigeons, ya know? But I'll see what I can do.'

I thanked him and told him I'd be in touch.

'I've got a sale on in a few months. Give me a call and when you leave make sure you mind that fuckin' dog.'

3

The Abramovich of Pigeon Racing

'Gerard Koopman is in the eyes of many wrapped in a shroud of mysticism. The extraordinary results that this man was able to accomplish in both breeding top pigeons and pigeon racing are probably sufficient to think about him in terms of a man with supernatural talents.'

Gerrit Van Eikenhorst, *Pigeon Paradise*

'Go in there and look for a tall bloke and a funny-lookin' fucker with glasses,' said Les over the phone. Les had a sore throat and he was running late.

It was a Sunday morning in mid-November and the Manchester sky was the colour of porridge. I was waiting outside the Renaissance hotel for Les and it looked as though it was about to rain. The pigeon-racing season had ended a month earlier and this was the time when Les earned his crust buying and selling pigeons at the numerous auctions he organized around the north-west.

'The funny-lookin' fucker with glasses' that Les had referred to was Gerard Koopman, aka The Flying Dutchman, who was arguably the best pigeon racer in the world. Gerard was Les's pal and Les was Gerard's agent in the UK. Basically, Les sold Gerard's pigeons in the UK and pocketed a small percentage from the sales.

I walked into the hotel and saw two men who fitted Les's flattering description. They were both standing with their hands in their pockets looking sheepish in the reception area, but rather than approach them and engage in awkward small talk I decided to hang around in the doorway and wait for Les.

He finally arrived half an hour late. When he pulled up Gerard and his pal were waiting for him.

'Hope you behaved yourself last night?' said Les to Gerard with a smirk.

Gerard laughed loudly, throwing his head back and forth. His long, pink shiny face turned crimson. Les introduced me to Gerard and his friend Andre. Gerard was dressed in a short black leather jacket and his small eyes peered through round tortoiseshell-framed spectacles.

We shook hands and swapped pleasantries and then we all climbed into Les's car and screeched off to the pigeon auction. Andre and Gerard sat in the back talking to each other in Dutch and Les chatted to me as though they weren't there.

'Couple of hillbillies these two fuckers,' Les said, pointing his thumb towards the back seat. 'From the countryside. Last time I went to visit him I got attacked by a herd of fuckin' cows,' he said, turning to look at Gerard accusingly.

Gerard lived in a small village called Ermerveen, in the far north-west of Holland, which consisted of just nine farms, and Andre lived several miles further north in a place called Drenthe. Gerard owned one of the nine farms and on it was an enormous pigeon loft which was home to some of the most prized racing pigeons in the world.

Racing pigeons had been in the Koopman family since the 1920s. Gerard's father, Cornelis, had been a successful racer and the pigeon-racing genes had been passed down to Gerard. 'There is no fancier alive that can stand in his shadow,' a journalist from *Pigeon Paradise* had written. Among many titles Gerard had won fourteen National championships, seven Olympiads and two World championships, and on top of the various baubles he'd made a small fortune selling 'feathered miracles' all over the globe — sometimes for as much as £10,000 a pigeon.

'He's like Abramovich,' said Les as we drove through a council estate on the outskirts of Manchester. 'He can buy anything he fuckin' wants. Isn't that right, Gerard?'

I turned around to look at Gerard. He smiled and looked confused.

'Isn't that right?' Les repeated.

It looked like Abramovich hadn't understood what Les had said, but he laughed anyway.

'He's one of the top flyers in the world, if not *the* top,' said Les looking serious and straight ahead at the road. 'You don't get much better than Koopman.'

Les took us on a scenic route through Pendleton, around the Salford Shopping City and past miles of austere and imposing rust- and charcoal-coloured high rise council blocks.

Gerard stared out of the window at the concrete tower blocks, the scowling teenagers wearing black tracksuits, and spindly old men with faces the colour of their intestines shuffling along clutching cans of turbo-strength lager.

'Where is the sale, Les?' Gerard gently enquired.

'Only the best for you, Gerard, my son. A

classy little place called the Steelworkers' Social Club in sunny Irlam.'

The Steelworkers' Club was set in a 1960s one-storey block surrounded by housing estates. A small group of middle-aged men were standing outside in the rain when we arrived. 'The door should be open, ye daft bastards,' Les shouted at them as we stepped out of the car. The men grumbled and then one of them tried the door and it opened. They muttered, groaned, and wiped their feet, walked into the club and we followed them in.

The formica tables and maroon velour-covered seats had been moved to the edges of the function room and underneath the Christmas decorations, the red and green thinning tinsel that hung from the polystyrene-tiled ceiling, were two long tables. On the tables were forty-five small white cages, each containing one of Gerard's pedigree pigeons.

'''ow are they lookin'?' said a fat man wearing a denim jacket that looked three sizes too small to another fat man wearing a dark blue Bolton Wanderers football top and a flat cap.

'They look well,' said the Bolton Wanderer. 'Some right big 'uns in there. Go well with the turkey at Christmas.'

Gerard had a permanently startled look on

his face and when he wasn't looking surprised, with lips puckered, he was laughing excitedly at Les or prowling around the function room with his hands in his pockets and a perfectly straight back, furtively eyeing the prospective buyers.

As he walked some of the men stared at the great pigeon man in their midst, and a small boy approached him to ask for an autograph and a photo.

The Abramovich of pigeon racing looked even more perplexed, maybe not understanding the request, but he mustered a nervous smile and stood with his arms at his sides as the boy inched in next to him and the camera flashed.

'Gerard'll do all right today,' said Les about his pal. 'We've already had some good bids in. Yeah, he'll do well and then he'll want me to take him on the fuckin' town. Won't you, Gerard?'

Gerard had his hand in one of the pigeon cages and he turned to look at Les while clasping one of the birds.

'He was out last night,' said Les. ' 'Take me to titty bars,' he said but I couldn't be bothered with all that. Him and Andre ended up on one of those bull riding machines in one of the boozers in town. They'd never seen anything like it. Everybody was laughin' at him. Specs all over the place. Fuckin' loved it. I think that's why he's walking a bit funny.'

The room was steadily filling up, mostly with men of forty years or over. They wore anoraks, leather bomber jackets, tracksuits and flat caps, and at least one of them was wearing all of those items at once. 'Fuckin' hell, the Scousers are in,' whispered Ray Lunt out of the side of his mouth.

Ray had just arrived and he was standing next to me as three pale, shaven-headed fat men strode in.

'All right, Ray?' one of the men said, and before Ray could reply they were standing at our table. They were keen pigeon racers from Liverpool and they laughed and joked with Ray for several minutes about the business, which was more than enough time for one of them to cajole me into buying a pigeon racing video for ten pounds. 'All the money goes to charity,' the man said as he handed me the video, entitled *Keep Them Healthy II*. I reluctantly handed him two crisp new five pound notes.

It wasn't midday yet but the bar was already ten deep with men talking pigeons. I squeezed my way in and ordered a drink. The barman stared at me as he poured the pint. With his barman's intuition he probably saw that I didn't look like a typical pigeon fancier.

'You with this pigeon lot?' he enquired with a slightly suspicious sneer.

I said I was but I wasn't a fancier. He looked bewildered at my answer and it was several minutes and several rounds of drinks later before he responded.

'It's fuckin' barmy. Buying a pigeon for £500? I wouldn't give you fifty pence for the lot. In fact there are a load on my roof. You can have them for nothing.'

I paid the barman, took my pint and sat back down with Ray. Les was standing on a small stage, testing the microphone as he warmed up for the sale. The room was now filled with around forty or fifty pigeon fanciers. They sat and chatted, opening the bird cages and checking out the pigeons. They looked at the wings, prised open the beaks and stared into the mouths of the pigeons. The pigeons didn't seem too concerned — they cooed a little faster and more excitedly but they didn't seem overly stressed by the manhandling.

'What are they looking for? Can you recognize a good pigeon from a bad pigeon just by looking at it?' I asked Ray.

'To be honest, all that is a load of fuckin' bollocks. There are all kinds of theories about what makes a winner but the main reason you win is if you work hard. Sometimes you can see fret marks on the feathers but these pigeons are as good as it gets. When our team look at a pigeon we just look at its feet to make sure it's got a good pair to land on.'

Ray introduced me to several other fanciers. 'Meet Albert. He's a character.' Albert looked a bit like Eric Sykes — he was tall, grey and a bit hang dog and miserable — and he was holding a well-thumbed piece of paper. 'He's a writer as well,' said Ray as I shook Albert's hand.

'Yeah, I sent this letter about pigeons and the way they are being treated in to the *Manchester Evening News* last week,' said Albert, heavy on the vowels like all Salfordians are.

'How are they being treated?' I enquired

'Fuckin' shit. As usual. Manchester council want to start using 'awks to get rid of the pigeons in the city centre. Problem with that is the 'awks will 'ave our pigeons too. It's always the same. People making it 'ard for us. We don't get the respect we deserve in this game.'

'Albert's a millionaire who's just come back from living in Newquay,' said Ray nudging me in the ribs when Albert had gone to the bar. 'He got bored down there with all that sun and money. Couldn't stay away from the pigeons.'

As well as Albert there was another millionaire in the room. Ray pointed to a bald man of around sixty-five who was wearing an old sheepskin coat and draining a pint at a table across from us. 'The maggot king . . . ' said Ray pointing to the man gulping on the pint. 'Maggots and budgerigars.'

'What do you mean?' I asked Ray.

'Made millions out of maggots and budgies,' said Ray looking at me as though I was stupid. I didn't know how to follow that so I left him and waited for the sale to begin.

I was on the lookout for a pigeon but Gerard's seemed a little out of my price range. Les told me that the cheapest would go for not much under £500 and the most expensive already had an online bid of nearly £6,000. I was told that was 'huge money' for young pigeons who were unproven.

Unproven or not though there were several big businessmen in the room keen to sample Gerard's wares and on the end of the phone there were several more. They included the Everton footballer Duncan Ferguson, who'd sent a friend along to do the bidding for him. Gerard was in demand. His birds were special. He dealt in the Ferraris of the pigeon world so it was just unfortunate that I had the budget for a Vauxhall Chevette.

The crowd were getting oiled and a little

impatient, with many taking long anxious drags on Drum roll-ups as Les looked for a new battery for the microphone.

Finally he announced the beginning of the sale. 'I think everybody knows the quality of these pigeons. These are not Mickey Mouse pigeons, fellas. These are some of the best young pigeons in the world.'

Within minutes the sale was in full flow and the money was changing hands quicker than one of Koopman's 'feathered miracles' on a windy day in Ermerveen.

'These are investments. Like buying a house. You can't lose money on these,' said Les, pointing to the grey birds in front of him. He looked imperious on the stage. He was the master of all he purveyed. He loved to perform and despite the sore throat and the dodgy microphone he commanded the stage with a swaggering authority.

The first bird went for £320 and the next for over five hundred. Not long into the sale the birds were selling for thousands.

'Direct from the famous Branco. Very well bred this one. A sister of Eric,' said Les about the grey hen selling as Lot 14. The sister of Eric was sold for just under £1,500, snapped up by a phone bidder.

'Half brother to Gazira,' said Les about another grey pigeon. 'Direct from Amira.'

'Is it a cock or a hen, Les?' said a Liverpudlian voice from a corner of the room.

'We've got it down as a cock but if you want it we can make it into a hen for you.'

The Scouser bought the pigeon for just under a grand. Two men were sat behind Les on the stage, one wearing a vest and woollen hat while the other man wore a permanent grin and a pair of stained jeans that were falling down around his waist to expose an ample backside. Once a pigeon was bought one of the men would stand and take the bird out of the white cage and box it up into a small red and blue Amtrak cardboard box with 'Homing Express' printed on the side. The box had a handle and several holes in it so the bird could breathe. Soon the floor and tables were scattered with the boxes stuffed with cooing pigeons.

The sale lasted for just under two hours and the big purchase of the day was Lot 25, another grey checker pigeon that looked, to me, like all the rest, but Les begged to differ. 'This is a unique bird . . . ' he said to the audience who were sat hushed and transfixed. 'There's a two-year waiting list to buy one of these. Pigeons like this don't come along every day.' I looked at the unique bird in its cage. It sat, blinking and twitching under a fog of cigarette smoke. 'This is a brother to Noble Blue,' Les continued. 'Direct from the Golden Lady . . . straight from the Kleindirk.'

This had me confused but the audience were buzzing in anticipation and soon the bids were pinballing around the function room as if lives depended on it. Four, five and six thousand pound bids were made for the pigeon until Les said, 'Sold to my friend over there!' and the pigeon was finally trousered by a skinny bloke with a moustache for £7,000.

'You've got a bargain there, my friend,' said Les as the bird was handed over. As the sale drew to its close I sat back and stared out across the function room. Behind the bar I could see the barman cleaning pint glasses and shaking his head.

Before I could stretch my legs Ray was back again. 'Good sale that,' he said. I nodded and then I asked him what made the birds so special. 'Well, Koopman did a thing that no one else had done. Years ago he crossed the Jannssens and the Van Loons and he was the first to do that.'

He smiled and folded his arms as though everything had become clear. I asked him to elaborate.

'There were great pigeons bred by a family called the Janssens and there were great pigeons bred by the Van Loons and he crossed 'em,' said Ray succinctly. I waited for more but none was forthcoming and before I could ask another question Ray was off and chatting with the 'maggot king'.

'When you're ready can you go and sex the pigeons?' a man with a lisp and a pint of Guinness said to Gerard. Some of the punters didn't know whether they'd bought a cock or a hen. They thought it would help to know. Gerard smiled and nodded. As well as that slightly perplexed look that he wore he now had an expression of barely concealed excitement. The grin was large and fixed. He was very happy and so was Les. I looked up to see him with his arm around the man who'd bought the pigeon for £7,000. Les was talking and laughing loudly.

I nodded and smiled in their direction and soon they were standing at my table along with the £7,000 pigeon.

'You don't want to lose that,' I said, pointing at the box.

The man with the moustache glanced at the box with the pigeon in. 'Ahm not fookin' bothered,' he said in a strong Geordie accent. Les laughed. The bird flapped around.

'He had a life-changing experience. He doesn't give a fuck. Do you?' said Les to the

Geordie. 'Doesn't give a shite,' Les continued, stressing the lack of care his pal had in the world. I grinned like a fool, but had no idea what he was talking about.

The Geordie nodded and took a long pull on his pint. Soon Gerard and Andre had joined us. Gerard had succesfully sexed the pigeons and now he and his friend were ready for a night on the town. 'Where are we going tonight?' asked Gerard.

'For a Chinese and home,' said Les.

'What about the titty bar?' said Gerard.

'Chinese for me and then offskie,' said Les.

Gerard and Andre looked a little disappointed before finishing their drinks and heading for the door.

The man with the £7,000 pigeon was swaying a little now and some of his pint was sloshing over the edge of the glass and onto the pigeon box.

'So what was the life-changing experience?' I asked before I left.

'He was blown up in the Bali bomb,' said Les, and the man nodded to confirm. 'It was nearly curtains. He told his missus he was in Dubai on business and instead he went to Bali and got fuckin' blown up by Al Qaeda.'

Les started to laugh and he carried on until he was coughing up some of the lager he was drinking. 'He got rescued by two Swedes. He was supposed to be in Dubai. Can you believe it?' Les repeated through the coughs.

'Aye, I live for the day now,' said the Geordie philosophically while steadying himself with his hand on the table. 'No point in fookin' worryin' now . . . When you've been blown up it makes you think what everythin's all aboot.'

'And what is it all about?' I asked.

'What's it all aboot?' he said, before picking up the pigeon box and peering through the holes. 'I don't fookin know. Shaggin' and pigeons, I suppose.' Then he picked up his seven grand pigeon and walked to the bar for another pint.

4

Zandy's Vision

'The one thing I console myself with is this: if you enter this race as a pigeon fancier, then you have the opportunity of months of pleasure in terms of racing your pigeon. If that is your reason for entering, you are already a winner when you start. If, however, you enter with the sole purpose of winning the race because you want to invest your entry fee so you could use the winnings to buy clothes for your kids, you shouldn't get involved. If that is your reason, don't enter the race.'

Zandy Mayer (SCMDPR race organizer)

It was Frank, Colin's granddad, who had told me about the race that afternoon in the pub even before Les had thrown it into the conversation months later. 'The Million Dollar race in South Africa . . . it's the World Cup final of one-loft races. The big one,' Frank had said, squinting after his fifth of eight pints of bitter. '$200,000 the winner gets, and the next few pocket a hundred grand each.'

As pigeon racing disclosures go, the revelation that a single bird could pocket you such a chunk of cash was a substantial one, but at the time the magnitude of the statement hadn't really registered. Frank was drunk and I was so preoccupied with finding Colin that I hadn't paid much heed to 'the big one', but all that changed the morning a brown envelope landed on my doormat.

The envelope had been sent second class and had taken nearly a fortnight to reach my hallway, sodden and half opened. I picked it up and unpeeled the torn edges to reveal a succinct message from Frank scrawled in blue biro. 'Might be interested in this,' the message said under a glob of tomato ketchup. The note was wrapped around a DVD and a folded sheet of A4 with the heading "THE 11TH SUN CITY MILLION DOLLAR (THE GREATEST PIGEON RACE IN THE WORLD). YOUR OFFICAL INVITATION TO ENTER THIS GREAT RACE.'

I read the A4 sheet with a giddy feeling in my stomach that I'd not felt since a childhood trip to a caravan site in Fleetwood, Lancs, had resulted in a runner-up spot in a competition to find the best under-twelve 'monkey impersonator'.

'Why not join us in paradise?' it said in bold black ink on the photocopied sheet.

Million quid? Paradise? This did indeed look like 'the big one'. I read quickly through the sheet and then slipped the half-hour trailer for the race into the DVD player and sat on the edge of the settee, hunched forwards and staring at the screen like a man who needed something, anything, to happen in his life.

Grainy images of men in bowler hats and thick moustaches struggling to start an enormous biplane propeller flickered across the screen before a plummy South African, who sounded like Donald Sinden, said: 'It's only been a hundred years since man conquered the skies. When the Wright brothers flew their heavy machine at Kitty Hawk in 1900.'

Charles Lindbergh appeared on screen shortly after, waving his cap to an adoring crowd after his historic solo transatlantic flight in 1927. He then faded from view and was quickly replaced by a shiny fighter jet dipping and spinning through perfect blue skies. 'Modern jet aircraft make use of satellite navigation systems that allow pin-point accuracy anywhere on the planet.' Suddenly I thought Frank had sent the wrong film, but the fighter jet was soon making way for the glorious image of a racing pigeon in flight.

'Modern flight has not diminished the awe

in which man holds the racing pigeon,' declared the South African Sinden.

Man holds the racing pigeon in awe? It was news to me but the pigeon-fancying hordes who were packed into an auditorium in a Sun City hotel certainly did. The film cut to thousands of pigeon lovers sitting in a place called the Super Bowl watching two huge screens for the first of 5,000 pigeons to return in the 2005 Million Dollar race. The camera panned around the auditorium, landing on many sweating, bespectacled faces chewing on their nails and gulping lager as they anxiously waited and hoped that one of their feathered wonders would be the first to return to the loft.

A man gave regular updates on the wind and weather conditions as Germans with fat pale legs mingled with hairy-armed South Africans frying curly sausages for men with St George tattoos. The clock ticked over to ten hours since the pigeons were released and the auditorium held its breath until the first bird landed, tiptoeing into the trap in the loft to trigger scenes something akin to Houston mission control on the day Armstrong landed on the moon. Light fittings vibrated from the noise of the cheers and applause, and men, women and children leapt out of their seats and embraced each other with moist-eyed

57

excitement as the birds reached the traps.

When the fixtures and fittings had settled, a phlegmatic American called Bob Kinney and his pigeon Four Starzzz Dream were revealed as the winners. Bob took it all in his long-legged stride, like a man who is familiar with pigeon racing glory. He wore a beanie hat and looked like Hunter S. Thompson. 'No other race compares with the Sun City Million Dollar' he said, before allowing himself a smile and accepting the fat cheque for $200,000.

There were many more winners and everyone was having a swell time, including a rank outsider in a white suit called Rodolfo who hailed from Mexico. 'Viva Mexico!' said Rodolfo as he collected his lolly. It went on. Many more cash prizes and cars were dished out to gleeful pigeon owners from Taiwan to Kuwait. 'But the Million Dollar race is not all about money,' said Sinden in conclusion. 'It's about a coming together of people and it's about pride in your pigeon.'

It's not all about money? I pondered what it was all about as I stared at a small mob of street pigeons which had suddenly landed under my window and were pecking and squabbling over a half-eaten carton of pie and chips that had been hurled into my back yard.

$200,000 for a pigeon race? In anybody's

book it was great money and with Les and his loft of winged wonders at my side we would surely have a decent chance of snaffling one of the cash prizes. $200,000 or even $2,000? What I couldn't do with a wad like that. My financial state was at best perilous. I was running on fumes, I needed dental work and a new overcoat, and my corned beef intake was becoming a worry to both my doctor and my mother. On top of that my social life didn't stretch much beyond the small walk up the hill to the local pub, where a big night out was several pints, a quiz, and a five foot two inch tribute act who called himself Derek Clapton. Things had been better, and to exacerbate the precarious situation my ex-girlfriend had called with the news that she'd found a new bloke and with her father's help they were buying a house together.

'And how are you?' she had said after relaying the good tidings about the new man and the house.

'Oh, I'm doing great. I've got something big planned.'

'Yeah?'

'Yeah. Real big, a chance to make myself some big money.'

'What's that?'

'Pigeon racing. I've bought a pigeon and I'm going to race him and win a hundred grand.'

She hadn't expected that. Who would? That had forced her onto the back foot. She had the big house coming? So what. I had my pigeons (or at least I would soon. That was no problem. I had Les Green on my side, and Les had loads of them).

'You've got no chance. Fuckin' no chance,' said Les down the phone.

I told him I wanted a piece of the 'big one', the Million Dollar race, but Les seemed adamant he wasn't going to get involved.

'But Les, what a prize! And with your loft of birds surely we'll take them to the cleaners?'

'Fuckin' no chance,' Les reiterated with the blunt intonation of someone who wasn't going to be budged. 'It's a lottery. You have no control over how your birds are trained. You send them over as young 'uns and they're looked after by loft managers over there. What's to stop them taking a backhander and making sure a South African pigeon wins? And not only that, you can fork out for a bird and then it gets eaten by a hawk or a fuckin' black mamba snake. Anything can go wrong. It's too much of a risk. How can anyone guarantee that you won't get fucked over in one way or another?'

I didn't have an answer to that but I had to find one. Les had to be persuaded. I genuinely thought that with a Les bird in the hand one of the big cash prizes could be won. Surely with the irresistible combination of a Koopmanbred and Les-trained winged miracle we were in with a shout? And even if we weren't I could see nothing else on the murky horizon that would raise the sort of money on offer at the million dollar pigeon extravaganza. I needed a little light in my life and with one of Les's birds I could see a flashing golden sliver of light cutting through the gloom. One of the first birds back in the loft and I could start dreaming of a year or two with the elusive luxury of solvency, plus time on my hands to work on something I didn't despise.

Outside South Africa, if you wanted to know anything about the Million Dollar race you spoke to Paul Smith. Paul was an ex-pigeon racer who now had the role of international coordinator for the race. His phone number was on the sheet Frank had sent.

'It's $1000 to enter three pigeons in the race,' Paul explained over the phone. 'And those birds are flown out to South Africa and trained by very experienced pigeon loft managers months in advance. It's all professionally done and everyone has an equal chance . . . if you know what I mean'.

Paul's Essex accent had a slight nasal drone and initially conjured up an image of an officious factotum intent on imposing a fine, but as we talked he seemed friendly and he clearly knew his stuff. He had an endearing habit of finishing each sentence with a pause before he tailed off with 'if you know what I mean'.

'A lot of people haven't got a clue about what we do,' said Paul before he rang off. 'They think pigeons are flying rats. But they are far from it. There've been some remarkable feats of endurance over the years from pigeons. They've flown across oceans and helped us win the war — a lot of people haven't got a clue about pigeons . . . if you know what I mean.'

Paul told me he would help in any way he could. He said the Million Dollar race was open to anyone who could cough up the money and the pigeons. I told him that sounded good and I arranged to meet him in Letchworth Garden City near to the village where he lived.

★   ★   ★

The sun was shining as I stood outside the clean and leafy train station in Letchworth. I arrived early and as I waited for Paul a man and a woman stumbled out of the station, disturbing the peace as they argued loudly over the ownership of a two litre bottle of White Diamond cider. They threw their arms about and shrieked like a couple of scraggy underfed gulls until the woman kicked out a thin leg and the cider went spinning into the air, crashing onto the tarmac before rolling under a car.

Letchworth was the brain child of the Victorian urban developer Ebenezer Howard. Howard thought our lives would improve if we lived on tree-lined streets surrounded by agricultural land. He thought the marriage of town and country was the way forward.

Paul Smith was a fan of the vast expanses of fields that spread through that part of Hertfordshire. Hertfordshire was where he grew up and where he flew his first pigeon. He stepped out of his car, smiled and shook my hand. He had a shy demeanour, a healthy, ruddy complexion and thinning silver hair. He looked a little like Butler's randy sidekick Jack from *On the Buses*, only stockier and with better teeth. 'You get all sorts round here . . . if you know what I mean,' he said as we drove away from the station and into the countryside.

Paul was born and raised in Letchworth and started flying pigeons in 1959. He flew them for over forty years until he retired to open up a pigeon stud and a company called Regency Lofts that sold pigeon paraphernalia such as medicines and cat deterrents. Paul was another pigeon success story. He had done well out of his feathered friends. He had a nice house in the country where he lived with his wife and he travelled the world promoting the Million Dollar race and another big money contest called the Europa Classic, held in Cardiff each year with a first prize of £30,000.

'Pigeons have been good to me, you could say,' said Paul as he drove us down narrow country lanes. 'I've met some wonderful people and been to places I'd never imagined. It just goes to show what pigeons can do for a person if you put the time and effort in.'

We eventually arrived at a thatched pub in a place called Barnston. The pub was Paul's local. 'It's several hundred years old,' he told me, although he didn't know exactly how old, 'and owned by a bloke who used to be in *London's Burning.*' We walked in. A few workmen in fluorescent green jackets eyed us with suspicion and we were greeted with a thin smile of polite indifference by a blonde barmaid with a face the colour of tinned ravioli. Paul ordered the drinks and a cheese and pickle sandwich, and we found a table.

Tractors rumbled by on the road outside as we pulled up a couple of seats under a framed England football shirt autographed by several members of the 1966 World Cup winning team. Paul seemed slightly distracted. He stared intently out of the window at the gleaming new cars coming and going from the car park. 'You get a lot of young couples in here at lunch time,' he said leaning forward conspiratorially. 'Meeting their boyfriends and girlfriends . . . if you know what I mean.'

I didn't know what he meant. 'A lot of people having affairs around here are there?' I offered.

Paul said nothing. He just sat back, took a bite of his cheese and pickle sandwich and raised an eyebrow. He seemed to take an interest in what other people were doing in and around his little village. He told me there'd been a murder in the area not long ago. 'It's a quiet little village . . . except for the odd murder,' he said, between bites of his sandwich.

I looked around at the patrons. Maybe Paul had a point. There did seem to be a touch of the P. D. James about the place. There were several straight-backed men sitting with pretty blondes and those country lanes looked perfect for a dogging session but I wasn't concerned about murder and the illicit activities of country folk. I had more pressing concerns — I wanted to know about pigeons and the big-money race.

'I wasn't always full time with the pigeons,' said Paul pulling his gaze away from the car park and focusing it on his pint. 'I worked making ladies' stockings. I was on the night shifts, and then I'd take care of the pigeons.' When he wasn't producing nylons, Paul, by all accounts, had been an excellent pigeon racer. He'd won 'positions in Nationals' and dominated clubs around Hertfordshire and Essex for most of the forty-odd years he'd spent in the loft. In fact he had been such a good racer, he told me, that several clubs had thrown him out. 'To give other fanciers a chance,' he said, before laughing. 'That happens a lot in this game. There's a lot of jealousy. There are blokes who couldn't fly kites on a windy day, and they are the ones who moan all the time instead of getting off their arses and doing something about it and working their pigeons. That's pigeon people for you, unfortunately.

'Basically I had nothing to prove any more

in the pigeon-racing game. I'd done everything I'd wanted to do. I'd had my share of success in the federation and elsewhere, and I'd won twenty-one gold medals at the pigeon Olympiad.'

Les Green had told me about the pigeon Olympiad. It was 'not his cup of char' apparently. 'It's like Miss World . . . only with pigeons,' Les snorted with a contemptuous sneer. 'A beauty contest . . . like fuckin' Crufts . . . load of shite, to be honest with yer.'

I have to say that Les, in his indomitably blunt and unforgiving style, was being rather harsh. The Olympiad is a popular event that attracted pigeon fanciers from all over the world. It is held every two years and (like Crufts I admit) the pigeons are judged on their pedigree, looks and handling. Paul had made a name for himself at the Olympiads and had managed the British team from 1983 to 1985. This was where he gained some of his notoriety as an excellent organizer and it was where he'd made his 'glamorous' pigeon-racing contacts. Paul was a friend of the former England footballer and pigeon fanatic Gerry Francis, as well as the South African businessman and former pigeon racer Zandy Meyer, the man who will go down in history as the creator of the Sun City Million Dollar classic.

'Zandy had a vision,' said Paul as the orange-faced barmaid's arm appeared in front of his face and began to remove the plate and empty glasses. 'He had a vision to create a pigeon race that was the equivalent to the two million dollar golf tournament in Sun City.'

'Only with one million?' I said.

'Only with one million. I'd been to more one-loft races than anyone else and so Zandy and I got together to make his vision a reality . . . if you know what I mean.'

This time I did. The one loft race would be closer to a horse race and so the pigeon ignoramus, such as me, would find it easier to understand, and a new, bigger audience could help revolutionize pigeon racing. Unlike the races Les and his pals took part in each Saturday, the one-loft race would see the pigeons released in the same spot and after several hundred miles — roughly 632 km for the Sun City race — arrive back at the same location. With its simple format the idea was for the race to appeal to a wider audience. Anyone could join in. You didn't have to spend weeks cleaning the loft and watching your birds chomp on barley. All you needed was a pigeon and you were in with a chance. Easy. But there had been problems. Some (like Les) were reluctant to join because of possible corruption. The first few races were dominated by South African flyers and some smelt a rat or at best a bit of pigeon jiggery-pokery.

'Of course you're bound to get the cynics,' said Paul quietly as he fiddled with a napkin. 'You are bound to get those who say there is fixing and corruption, but it's simply not true. The good thing about the Million Dollar race is that all the rings on the birds are covered with a tamper-proof seal so no one knows where the birds are from. The loft managers who do the day-to-day work don't know if the pigeon is from South Africa, or Ireland, or wherever. And the staff are all on bonuses not to lose any pigeons, so there is no danger of any of them going walkabout. It's all very professionally run and it's doing very well. You wouldn't get the numbers that you do competing in the race if they thought that the race was fixed in any way.'

Paul was a big fan but then he helped to run it and had won second place and over one hundred grand in 2001. Over five thousand competed in 2006, and Paul and Zandy expected at least that to compete in 2007. The race was a success and turning over a tidy profit as well as now attracting a better class of fancier. 'We've got the Queen's birds competing in the next race. She has a pigeon loft although I'm not sure how keen a fancier she is. We've let her compete for PR purposes. It's a nice thing to say that the Queen is competing in your pigeon race.'

I didn't disagree but it wasn't HM that I wanted to see in the race, it was Les Green. 'I hope you can persuade Les to compete,' said Paul as we left the pub and walked to his car. 'I know that he and his partners are keen as mustard, and top-class racers. They are the sort of people we want in the race. The best racers around.'

I told Paul that Les was going to take some talking round. Les liked to be in control of his birds. They were first-class pigeons and they were worth money and, better than that, prestige. He didn't want to risk his birds being neglected, or eaten by a snake. If Les didn't fancy sending his beloved birds over several continents maybe there was another big-money race closer to home.

'Nothing to compare with that race. Not in terms of both money and prestige,' said Paul as we drove back to Letchworth.

'Someone else tried to compete with our race and set up his own million dollar pigeon event,' he told me as we pulled into the station. 'It was the guy who won the race when I came second. He thought it was easy money and he tried to get me involved but I

70

said no way. Anyway, it all went pear-shaped.'

'What happened?' I said as I stepped out of the car.

'The organizer ran off with the money . . . if you know what I mean.'

5

Mike Tyson and the Birmingham Rollers

'Standing here and watching them flying around free is one of my favourite things. They're very soothing and they keep me out of the strip clubs.'

Mike Tyson

Mike Tyson was on his way to Britain for a week-long after-dinner speaking tour. The former heavyweight champion of the world and self-confessed pigeon fanatic was in need of money, having blown an estimated $400 million in just over twenty years as a pro boxer. He was in the process of recovering and piecing together the emotional rubble and mountain of debt that had accumulated from a fractured life and career.

Flying to Britain and speaking in hotels and function rooms in London, Birmingham, Manchester, Derby and Doncaster (for an estimated £150,000 per night) about the extreme highs and lows of his life, both in and out of the ring, was part of that process of recovery. 'I feel a lot of love from the people of England. I think of it as my second home,' Tyson told *USA Today* before he was due to leave for the UK.

'Tyson is coming to Manchester!' said Les over the phone, with the sort of excitement he usually reserved for the pigeons. Les was a big boxing fan and most boxing fans secretly had a soft spot for Tyson.

I told him I was aware of it but I had also heard that in true Tyson fashion he was liable to pull out of the trip at any minute.

'He's definitely coming,' said Les with great certainty. 'And a bloke I know is helping to organize it.'

The bloke Les was talking about was the boxing promoter Wally Dixon and Wally, Les assured me, was 'a big pigeon man'. Apparently Wally would have some say in what Tyson did, if and when he came to the UK.

'Wally reckons that Tyson is looking to buy some pigeons and have a look at a few lofts while he's over here.'

'You're going to sell pigeons to Mike Tyson?'

'I don't know about that but Wally reckons he might be able to bring him up to the loft. Tyson in the loft. That'll be all right, won't it?'

Les was relishing the prospect of 'brewing up' for Tyson and his cronies. And as unlikely as it sounded, it did seem remotely possible. Wally Dixon was a friend of Ray Fisher, and Fisher was the Manchester businessman who had spent around a year organizing the Tyson trip. The word was out that Tyson liked Fisher and didn't want to let him down. Although professing to like someone had never stopped Tyson reneging on a deal before, Les said that Wally was sure that Mike was going to honour the deal he had struck with Fisher.

'You can't deny that he's a legend,' said Les before he hung up. 'You can't take that away from Tyson. And he's a mad pigeon man.' Mad was maybe the key word in Les's summary.

Like Les I also had a certain nostalgic soft spot for Tyson, but I wasn't sure whether I'd want him around my pigeon loft, if I had one, or anywhere else for that matter. Tyson had been an outstanding fighter during his prime: from the moment in 1986 when he'd knocked Trevor Berbick senseless to become the youngest heavyweight champion, to the point at which he beat Frank Bruno in the fifth in 1989, despite Bruno's clubbing right uppercut in the first round.

Tyson had combined speed, power and intimidation better than any heavyweight fighter I'd seen, and at the peak of his powers he would, arguably, have troubled any heavyweight in history, including Muhammad Ali and Joe Louis. Sadly those ring achievements, way back in the eighties, had long been overshadowed by the predictable and depressing catalogue of crimes and misdemeanours that Tyson had piled up, to the point where they were so distant they hardly mattered.

Tyson had been raised in fatherless poverty in Brownsville — a brutal ghetto of Brooklyn, New York — and long before he was convicted of raping the beauty queen Desiree Washington in 1992 (which to all intents and purposes finished him as a top-level fighter), and before the rapacious fight-promoter Don King had crowbarred himself into Tyson's life, he had had his share of trouble.

Tyson had always carried with him a sense of injustice and a chip on his shoulder the size of the Empire State building. He was always likely to explode into a fit of rage, if at all disturbed. It was a rage born in that ugly Brownsville ghetto and it was partly forgivable when he was a struggling teenager, but somewhat laughable (if it hadn't been so destructive and damaging to all concerned) when he was a multi-millionaire boxing champion with several mansions and a fleet of Ferraris.

That lack of control and blind rage first reared its ugly head in a childhood incident concerning the death of one of Tyson's beloved pigeons. Tyson had kept pigeons since he was nine years old. For a dollar or two he would clean the pigeon coops of local fanciers: he enjoyed the gentleness and quiet elegance of the pigeon. 'When I saw the birds I just fell in love with them, and after a while I would take the birds in exchange for cleaning the coops.' Later in his life Tyson would say that he enjoyed the peace and calm of the pigeons and the loft.

When Tyson was around ten years old he was approached by an older boy who was a notorious local gang member, and while Tyson was playing with his pigeons the older boy snatched one of the birds. Tyson pleaded with the boy to return it but the boy mocked him and then slowly began to turn the head of the pigeon, in front of Tyson, until the bird's head snapped off. Burning with anger the ten-year-old Tyson — who probably weighed around 160/170 pounds even then — took his revenge by tearing into the boy and smashing him with kicks and punches until the boy lay unconscious on the floor. And this was not the only violent incident concerning Tyson's love of pigeons.

When he was a little older he awoke one morning to find his favourite pigeon Julius had died. 'I was devastated,' he said in an interview years later. 'And I was gonna use his crate as my stick ball bat to honour him. I left his crate on my stoop and went to get something and I returned to see the sanitation man putting the crate into the crusher. I rushed him and caught him flush on the temple with a titanic right hand. He was out cold, convulsing on the floor like an infantile retard.'

Tyson continued, 'A pigeon fancier is very caring. There is a great gentleness about them when they handle the pigeons and it is a very sensual thing.'

He also said, when his career was drawing to a close, that the pigeons were his next love after his kids. He was addicted to them 'like a degenerate'.

At the height of his career Tyson had 4,000 birds at the mansion he owned in Harlem and often spent over $1,000 a week on them, sometimes much more, and when it came to pigeons he said he often took better care of them than he did of himself.

Tyson arrived in the UK for his speaking tour in early November 2005. Around 500 people paid £100-200 each to see him and hear him speak at a second-rate hotel called the Heritage in Derby on a cold and damp night. According to the many newspaper reports the day after, Tyson was gushing with praise for his English fans. 'I never thought I'd experience anything like the love in this room,' he said, before answering questions from the audience. Tyson did what he had to do and the night went without a hitch, apart from a drunken scuffle in the dining area after he had left the building. The following day I received a phone call from a newspaper editor who had been told I had an interest in both boxing and pigeon racing.

The editor confirmed what Les had told me weeks earlier. Tyson was on the look-out for pigeons while he was in the UK, and the editor wanted to know if I could write a story on Tyson in the pigeon loft.

'There's a chance he'll be coming to see a friend of mine,' I revealed, 'at a loft in Oldham.'

That was it. I had a commission. The editor liked the idea of Tyson meeting Les and I liked the idea of writing for a good paper and the money, even though it wasn't much, would be a godsend. I was low on cash as usual and it would see me through Christmas. With a sense of urgency I got on to Les.

'Not heard back from Wally yet,' said Les with a little less excitement than the last time we'd spoken.

'Tyson will be in Manchester in a couple of days. When will you know?' I said, slightly panicked.

'Wally said he would ring as soon as he knew anything. Should be any time soon,' said Les.

Tyson wasn't a pigeon racer as such, not like Les and the gang. He kept the sort of birds that Les referred to as 'fancy' pigeons — he had around 350 of various breeds at his home in Phoenix, Arizona, and knew all of them by name. He kept pigeons called Rollers and Tumblers, as well as other more exotic breeds. They were bred for their looks — they could be coloured in beautiful pastel shades known as cream checker, brown almond and spread faded brown — and for their aerial acrobatics and short spectacular bursts of energy, rather than their stamina, speed and vitality, which was what the racing pigeon was bred for.

Tyson's favourite breeds of pigeon were supposedly the Birmingham Rollers and the Deep Rollers. The Deep Rollers were a rather unpredictable pigeon as they wouldn't always roll, and no one knew for sure why they rolled in the first place, but they were a spectacular breed of pigeon. Both types of roller could fly up to a thousand feet high, sometimes more, and suddenly nosedive into a deep, seemingly death-defying roll, kamikaze style, just a whirring ball of feathers hurtling down towards the ground, until they pulled themselves to safety at the last moment. Don Lehman, the chairman of the American roller club, described them thus: 'A Birmingham roller rolls for about three seconds; it rolls very tight and very straight. And then the deep rollers from Kent in England roll much further, often for up to seventeen or twenty seconds, but they don't spin as tight. From what I can gather, it's almost like an epileptic fit they have that puts them into the roll, and what happens is that the Birmingham roller rolls a lot more often in a ten-minute period (it may roll up to five times) while a deep roller may only roll once. The deep roller climbs much higher because of the depth of the roll and the other roller yo-yos more. It moves like roll — stop — up, roll — stop — up. When pigeons roll together, they call it a kit. They do it synchronized like swimming. The tumbler and the tippler, the American high flier, the German high flier; they all have their own games.'

It was a strange and wonderful sight if you liked that sort of thing, and Tyson did — he adored them. So much so that he'd attended pigeon racing meetings in Phoenix, and even appeared at a council meeting to offer his support for the local fanciers of Phoenix in a dispute over how many pigeons they were allowed to keep. In fact the obsession was so strong he had even hired a hotel room next to his for eight of his rollers before the fight with Danny Williams in Louisville, Kentucky in 2004, although the calming presence of the birds didn't do him much good as Williams stopped him in the fifth.

'The deep roller is what Mike Tyson has been,' said Tyson's therapist Marilyn Murray, who first met him in 1999 when he was receiving intensive sex therapy. 'He's a guy who doesn't take the normal tumbles like the average person.'

Before Tyson's date at the Hilton hotel in Birmingham, he made an unlikely stop at the Warley Roller Pigeon Society in Bloxwich, Walsall, to thank a pigeon man called Horace Potts for introducing him to the Birmingham roller — which had been bred in Birmingham in the 1800s. Horace had been a pigeon man for many years in the Midlands and he appreciated the call from Tyson, who turned up wearing a leather flying jacket and a Russian hat. 'You can tell he loves these birds,' Horace told the gathering crowd as

Tyson cradled and kissed a Birmingham roller. 'Look at the way he looks at them — he really shows an interest.'

Tyson went down well in Birmingham and at Horace's place. He was behaving himself and he appeared to be in relatively good spirits. Maybe it was the blonde he had on his arm each evening that was keeping his spirits up, or maybe it was the pigeon videos he insisted on watching in the limo as he drove from venue to venue. Anyway, if he was in fine fettle and he'd made a trip to a pigeon loft in Walsall, surely Les was in with a shout of receiving Tyson's ample presence in Oldham. Maybe my fortune was changing after all. An exclusive with Tyson in the loft was now looking like a distinct possibility, or at least that's what I thought.

A couple of days before the Manchester date I rang Les to see if there'd been any word from Wally.

'It's off,' Les snapped.

'The night in Manchester, or Tyson at your loft, or both?'

'Tyson coming to see me. It's off. He wanted money to come up here to my loft. Can you fuckin' believe that? Wanted to get paid to come up to the loft. Fuck that!' said Les.

'So that's that?'

'As far as I'm concerned it is. I'm not that desperate for the attention that I'd pay Mike fuckin' Tyson to pay me a visit. Bollocks to that.'

I could see Les's point and I agreed with him. It was a bit rich — or desperate — of Tyson's people to ask for money (if indeed they had). And why would Les lie? Les was right to refuse to pay but the sudden Tyson no-show had loused up my story. I cursed my luck before I settled on a consolation prize of a free ticket from Les to go and see Tyson speak.

Tyson was due to appear at Old Trafford on a Saturday night in late November and I still had it in mind to grab him for a talk about pigeons and boxing. I had a vague idea that I might be able to offload a Tyson interview for a few hundred quid if Wally Dixon could give me any kind of access. It was worth a go.

'Good luck with that,' said Les sarcastically after I told him what I was planning to do. 'Without any money I think you'd have more chance of spending time with Elvis.'

Elvis certainly might have been easier to contact than Wally Dixon. Wally was well and truly incommunicado as I tried to get an 'in' with Tyson. The promoter Ray Fisher, though contactable, didn't give me much hope of spending any time with Tyson.

'Come down and ask a question from the floor after the dinner. That's probably the best thing to do,' said Ray, sounding like he was in a hurry to get me off the phone.

The event took place in a large function room inside the Old Trafford football stadium. I arrived at seven p.m. and there were around a thousand paying punters stuffed into a large, stuffy low-ceilinged room and most of them seemed to be half drunk already. The six or seven shaven-headed men sitting at my table certainly were.

'Park your arse and 'ave a fuckin' drink,' said a man who introduced himself as 'The Monk'.

'Are you mates of Les?' I enquired, pulling the lager towards me and taking an extra-long gulp.

'Les who?' They didn't have a clue who Les was.

'Tyson fans?' I enquired.

'I'm just here for the piss up,' said one of The Monk's pals in between drinks.

Tyson finally arrived an hour or so late and to rapturous applause from most, but boos from The Monk and his mates, which aroused a lot of violent looks from various members of the crowd, as the Rocky theme

84

played loudly and disco lights flashed across the muggy room.

Tyson was wearing a light grey double-breasted suit with a white shirt and dark tie, and he looked pretty good as he raised his hand and smiled while he took his seat at the top table next to Frank Bruno, Ray Fisher and several others.

Crowds of people, including The Monk and the other men at my table, rushed up looking for a picture or an autograph, or just a good gawp at Tyson. Most were stopped by a security rope and several unsmiling security men who were twice the size of the ex-champion.

I watched as The Monk and his pals were forced back while others queued up for a snap.

'Anyone going up to the rope uninvited will be evicted!' said the already irate compère over the mic.

The Monk and his pals weren't happy when they returned. They had paid over £100 each and they wanted a photo with Tyson for the wall of the insurance firm where they worked.

You had to pay £200 for a VIP ticket, they reckoned, and 'only the VIP fuckers get a photo'.

'Maybe you'll get the picture later,' I said,

trying to bring a little cheer into his life.

'He can kiss my arse now,' snarled The Monk.

The night got started and it was a mediocre affair. There were bad jokes and ordinary food and there was an auction of various bits of Tyson tat which were bought for wildly inflated prices by several of the wealthier lagered-up members of the crowd. It wasn't great and The Monk and his pals were getting increasingly drunk and obnoxious. I contemplated throwing in the towel but on my way to the bathroom I met Tom Patti.

Patti was an ex-fighter, a part-time actor and one of Tyson's pals from Cus D'Amato's training camp in the Catskill Mountains. I introduced myself.

'Having a good night?' Tom enquired.

'Not really,' I said, and explained my predicament. I told him I'd been trying to scrounge a bit of time with Tyson to talk pigeons. Tom was friendly and said, 'Mike loves pigeons. I'm not sure but I'll see what I can do.' And I returned to the room feeling a little better.

After what seemed like a very long time the microphone was eventually passed around the room for questions from the floor. Tyson hugged kids and answered the questions to earn his dough. Most of the questions were uninspired — of the 'what was your toughest fight' variety — but so were some of his answers. But what did I expect? I had a free ticket and on the whole it was good-natured and entertainment for some.

'Would you rather be a pigeon or a hawk?' said a man from somewhere in the room, after Tyson had answered several questions about boxing.

'The pigeon is the only bird that relies on men to look after it, and the hawk doesn't need man or anyone else,' said Tyson in a roundabout way after rambling for some time. He didn't say which he'd rather be but he said that 'the hawk is a natural predator with sharp instincts for survival. The pigeon lacks a ruthless streak.' So it appeared obvious which was closer to his character.

The night limped on and most of the punters seemed happy to be in the same room as Tyson, they didn't seem to mind if the questions were good or not, although The Monk did and after a while he began to chip in.

'What was your best punch?' a fat man in a black shirt had asked Tyson.

'The one he hit his wife with,' shouted The Monk.

'What makes you happy these days?' someone else asked.

'Rape,' shouted The Monk.

It wasn't good and it got worse. Sitting at the top table with Tyson and Bruno was a very large pale man called Joe Egan. Egan was one of Tyson's former sparring partners, and Tyson called him 'the baddest white man on the planet.' After The Monk had called out 'Rape!' he scowled in our direction and didn't look amused. And in a short time our table was visited by several large men, who, I presumed, were friends of Egan. They were polite but The Monk wasn't, and this didn't bode well for any of us.

'I'm not with that bunch,' I said to the thick-necked man, as he escorted me outside into the freezing cold. 'If you speak to Tom Patti he'll tell you. I'm waiting for him to get back to me. I just want to talk with Mike about pigeons.'

As we stood in the orange glow of the night I thought I saw a flicker of a smile and a hint of sympathy on the man's face. Maybe it was just a dodgy street light.

'If you don't fuck off I'll smack you so hard you'll be flying with the pigeons,' he growled.

At that point I realized I probably wouldn't be talking to Mike Tyson that night, so I said goodbye and headed into the cold.

6

Moonie's Return

'The Old Blue Cock'
Did the birds of prey,
Have their wicked way;
And tore him apart,
Which broke his heart;
Perhaps a blue hen did he meet,
Who was walking in the street;
I hope that one day,
He will come back to stay;
For he was my rock,
The old blue cock.

C.Cottle, *British Homing World*

At times I thought I might be losing my marbles. There had to be a more straightforward way of earning a few quid than attempting to enter a pigeon race, but Frank assured me that I wasn't and there wasn't.

'You've got the bug, that's all, kid,' said Frank with a wonky smile, once again several sheets to the wind. 'The pigeon bug. It happens to us all sooner or later.'

I doubted that it did, and I doubted that I actually had it, but due to the lack of anything else on the horizon I went along.

'There's no need to pay those sort of prices either,' said Frank, raising his glass and nodding reassuringly after I'd filled him in on the sale of the Koopman pigeons. 'Seven grand for a pigeon? They must be off their nappers paying that sort of dough. Listen, there's an old mate of mine who used to be a great flyer. You can 'ave a word with him. He'll come in with yer and you can 'ave some of his birds for nothing . . . or next to nothing anyhow.'

Frank's old pigeon pal was called Moonie. Moonie, Frank told me, had been something of a star racer in the 1970s. His birds had won federation honours and been placed in Nationals until, as the story goes, he was forced out of pigeon racing for chinning a club chairman at a Christmas party in 1979, after a long-running feud over missing funds from a charity raffle.

Moonie had been a good pigeon racer but in Frank's words he had, at one time or another, 'pissed everyone off'. Moonie had been something of a hellraiser, a loose cannon often fuelled on Holt's bitter and whisky chasers, and always liable to explode at the slightest bump in the path.

'Oh, he was a rum 'un was Moonie,' said Frank, puckering his lips and sucking in the smoky air to emphasize the threat that his mate had once posed. 'And nuttier than a squirrel turd.

'I suppose he was a bit like Georgie Best or Hurricane Higgins in some ways. Brilliant at what he did but he was a rum bugger and a bit of a pisshead. He had that Irish thing as well, that contempt for authority. He hated being told what to do, did Moonie, and he had a mouth on 'im like a ragman's trumpet.'

Moonie, Frank continued, had basically made 'a right tits up' of his promising pigeon-racing career. The sporadic violent outbursts and the mouth 'like a ragman's trumpet' had alienated him from his fellow flyers, and according to Frank he'd voluntarily walked the plank rather than play by the rules of the pigeon racing authorities. The impetuosity and rank stupidity of youth, or, in the case of Moonie, middle age, had apparently cost him pigeon racing immortality.

'Oh, he was a fuckin' balloon. He had the pigeon racing world at his feet but he made a right pig's ear of it,' said Frank. 'But he regretted it and I think it's haunted him ever since. Like Best never playing in the World Cup, Moonie thinks he's missed out on something.' And Frank reckoned I was the man to rekindle the minor conflagration that was Moonie and his racing pigeons.

Frank reckoned things had changed. Moonie's hair-trigger temper and raging thirst had now receded along with his curly ginger hair. Moonie had stopped howling at the moon. He'd mellowed in his old age — he was nearly seventy-five — and he was dreaming of a comeback.

'He was cast out like Lazarus,' said Frank dramatically, just before the bell for last orders. 'But now he is ready to return. The revenge of Moonie!' he added theatrically. 'Moonie returns!'

It sounded like a Hammer horror movie. I laughed and told Frank that Lazarus wasn't cast out, he rose from the dead. Frank took a gulp of his drink and shook his head as though I hadn't got the point.

'When you and Moonie get together and win that race it'll be as though he has risen from the dead.'

I could have laboured the biblical inaccuracy but I chose not to as it was getting on, so against my better judgement and somewhat pie-eyed (most of the decisions I now made regarding pigeons were under the influence), I agreed to ring Moonie to discuss the possibility of us joining forces to take on the world's best pigeon racers in Sun City.

'When I ring what shall I call him?' I enquired before I left.

'Moonie,' scoffed Frank, as though I was an idiot.

'But what's his real name?'

Frank squinted and thought for several seconds.

'Just call him Moonie.'

There was no voice on the end of the phone and all I could hear was the sound of a dog barking in another room. Then the bark got closer until I could hear the canine breathing down the phone, in between the barks. This went on for several minutes until a gruff Mancunian voice (that wasn't the dog) said, 'Who's that?'

I told him who it was, how I'd got the number and what I wanted.

The barking stopped but nothing else came back down the line until the fag-singed voice that I presumed was Moonie's said succinctly, 'I'll meet you in the Star.'

The Star was a pub on the outskirts of a large council estate near Whitefield in North Manchester. Some of the locals called it 'Fort Apache' due to the regular weekend battles and sieges. I'd been there once or twice before, as a teenager, and had once witnessed a pitched battle in the car park between a dozen or so fairground workers and the drivers from a local cab firm.

It was a small, square red-brick block that had been built sometime in the 1960s to lubricate the council estate dwellers and the workers who did something with foam in the factory close by. The factory had been demolished and the Star now stood in the middle of a piece of derelict land like a goitre on a cadaver.

The pub traditionally attracted the hard-core drinker and the mundanely insane — on a bad day it attracted the mundanely insane hardcore drinker. It was the sort of place where sober women under the age of sixty were seldom seen and the younger, predominantly male clientèle were, in Frank's words, 'all fuckin' head the balls'.

I walked into the Star and the smell of wet dogs, bitter slops and knock-off tobacco slapped me around the chops. It hadn't changed much since I was last there in 1988, except for maybe a few more stains in the green and yellow carpet. It had a low ceiling, which made it dingy and uncomfortably warm, and the six or seven patrons, who sat on their own in various nooks and crannies looked like they all had the potential for at least one murder before the day was out.

I ordered a drink from a surly barman with

a nose like a large, flaking, mummified strawberry and stood at the bar listening to the tinny plink-plonk of a *Coronation Street*-themed fruit machine that a grey-faced youth was ferociously feeding with pound coins. Then I felt a firm poke in the middle of my back.

'Are you the bloke?' said a throaty north Manchester voice.

I turned around quickly with a mixture of fear and irritation to see an old bald man, no bigger than five foot two, standing behind me holding a walking stick in one hand and the lead of a sad-eyed, hairy mongrel in the other.

'Are you the bloke?' repeated the man with a voice that didn't match the stature.

'What bloke?' I said.

'The pigeon bloke.'

I smiled with relief and said that I was, and the man introduced himself as Moonie before introducing the dog as Gregg.

'That's with two G's,' said Moonie, as though I'd had the temerity to suggest otherwise. 'Named after the great Manchester United goalkeeper Harry Gregg.'

I suggested a quick exit but Moonie had other plans.

'I'll 'ave one and then we'll bugger off,' he said, pointing his stick at the bar. Lacking any better offers I nodded in agreement and got the drinks in.

After the initial stick-poking introduction Moonie seemed friendly, if a little melancholy and cagey. 'My name's Tom but I'd prefer if you called me Moonie.' Moonie told me he hailed from Sligo but had lived and worked nearly all his life in England, mostly as a navvy on the railways, and now considered himself an honorary Mancunian. His father had flown pigeons from a young age back in Ireland but Moonie had come to them later than most. 'I wanted to be a footballer, that was my first love, but I was fuckin' useless. I got into the pigeons when I realized I wasn't going to play for Manchester United,' he said with a throaty laugh. 'And look where I am today.'

Moonie lived just a short walk from the pub in a semi-detached council house with a wild overgrown garden. His wife, Irene, had died several years before and on the way up to the house he told me he had stopped caring about mowing the grass and such things.

'It drives the neighbours mad,' he said as we stepped into his house. 'What with the garden and the pigeons, but fuck 'em. People 'ave got too much to say for themselves about other people's business these days. It's got to the point where you can't do anything without somebody complaining and calling the authorities. You can't even fart in peace around here.'

As well as the pigeons and Gregg the dog, Moonie lived with an African grey parrot called Lou — named after the former Man U centre forward Lou Macari. The parrot lived in a cage under a picture of Eric Cantona and a garish print of the Virgin Mary. As I approached it Moonie told me not to get too close as 'it had a vicious streak'. 'A little bastard he is,' said Moonie as he took his coat off. 'Got me into trouble a few months back, didn't ye, Lou?' he said, poking his fingers into the cage.

Apparently Lou had bitten the hand of a ten-year-old boy who lived next door and a feud had raged ever since. 'The little bugger was tormenting him but what can you do? Wasn't Lou's fault,' said Moonie with a shrug.

As well as the penchant for biting children, Lou the parrot had another string to his gaily feathered bow. In his spare time, and much to his own amusement, Moonie had taught the bird how to swear.

'Up yer tits!' the parrot shrieked, flapping with what seemed to be great excitement as Moonie rooted through cupboards looking for newspaper clippings of his past pigeon-racing successes. 'Moonie's got a big one!' the parrot squawked several minutes later. Moonie stopped rooting for a second, turned to me and laughed. 'Took me ages to get it to do that,' he said rather proudly, before delving back into a vast box of papers.

The house was untidy. Newspapers, cups, cans and plates were scattered around on the floor as well as on the small coffee table in the middle of the room.

'It's a bit of a tip. A woman pops round to help me clean up,' said Moonie apologetically as he rummaged around the cupboards. 'But she hasn't been in for a bit.' I told him that it didn't matter about the clippings and that he could find whatever he was looking for another time.

After much foraging Moonie finally gave in and led me out into the back garden to the loft. The garden was very overgrown and the three-foot-high grass was littered with rubbish, but Moonie didn't seem to mind.

'I'll sort this out in the summer,' he said with an air of nonchalance. 'Or maybe not. When you get to my age you get past caring.'

At the bottom of the garden was a small L-shaped loft that Moonie told me contained twenty pigeons. By the look of it, it was all that Moonie now cared for, apart from the dog and the parrot. The loft was cleaner than Moonie's front room and the birds hardly fluttered as we stepped in.

'A friend of mine left me these birds in his will.' Moonie carefully prised a handsome red pigeon from its hole. 'It feels good to have the pigeons back, to be honest. Irene was never that keen; she thought I spent too much time with 'em but I love having them around.'

Moonie shuffled around the loft feeding the pigeons and introducing me to them one at a time. 'This is Grace,' he said, holding a grey checker, 'and that's Sligo Lightning,' he said, pointing to another bird that looked very similar to the one he was holding. Moonie had twelve cocks and eight hens and they were good pigeons. 'Bred from Janssens . . . the great Belgian pigeon-racing family, all under two years old.' Most were grey checkers but there were a couple of reds and a fine looking black spread — so called because the black spread over the entire body.

It was early December, a rest period for the pigeons when they moult and begin to grow new feathers. Moonie said that he had the pigeons on rations because they didn't get the same exercise in winter and he didn't want them to get too fat.

'You've got to have good preparation before a racing season,' he said. 'Make sure you have them right. I sometimes don't let them out during the day in the winter. Maybe just for a bit of a fly around in the afternoon.'

After Moonie had finished the feed he led me out of the loft. As he was locking the door he was suddenly hit on the head with a blue balloon filled with water. It was sudden and quite startling in its own tragicomic way, and the water drenched Moonie. He reeled back a little, shocked, and said, 'Fuckin' bastards.' Instinctively I moved towards him to see if he was all right and as I did I was hit in the chest by a fat purple one. I was suddenly soaked.

'It's next door's fuckin' kids,' said Moonie in a panic, shaking some of the water off himself. I looked up and two teenage boys were hanging out of a second-floor window next door. They were laughing and whistling.

Moonie shouted at them and the boys hurled another water bomb which missed us but crashed onto the roof of the loft.

'Little fuckers!' he shouted, and the boys laughed and closed the window.

'You know what that's about, don't ye?' said Moonie as he closed the loft. 'That's all because of that fuckin' kid's hand and the bastard parrot.'

Moonie wasn't happy and vowed revenge for our soaking, but when he had calmed down and we'd both dried off he told me that he didn't want to waste his energy on anything but pigeons. He still had some of his old hunger for success, even though he was touching seventy-five and he said that he still had the desire to have a competitive loft. He wanted to race again. He planned to keep a small efficient loft of around twenty or thirty pigeons and he was interested in competing in one or two of the big one-loft races, even though he thought they were something of a con.

'You pay a lot of money to enter those races and the chances of your birds taking part in the race, let alone being there on the day they are liberated, are slim. But at my time of life you get to a point where it doesn't matter if you lose a few quid or a few birds. I'll help you out with a few pigeons if you need them,' he added kindly.

I liked Moonie and I was pleased to have him on board. Les Green was a pro and something of a pigeon racing genius, but I thought Moonie might be more my level. He wasn't after world domination, just wanted to be a part of something again. He wanted to be busy and away from the house and if he could make any money then that was a bonus. We would make a good team. He moved at my pace, certainly in terms of the pigeons anyhow, and he was also happy to put up a couple of pigeons for nothing.

We shook on the partnership several days later over drinks in the Star. Moonie would provide the pigeons and the expert knowledge, and I would provide the entrance fee to the South African race. If we won anything we would split it down the middle fifty-fifty. Moonie seemed happy and so was I. I now had the pigeons, or at least I would have the pigeons very shortly, when Moonie's birds began to mate.

Just before Christmas I called Moonie several times to wish him the best for the festive season. But each time there was no reply. He's at the Star or with relatives, I thought, and I enjoyed my Christmas break safe in the knowledge that in the new year I'd be joining forces with him and we would at least be in the mix as far as the money races were concerned.

I called Moonie again shortly after the holiday. We had arranged to meet early in January to make plans and organize a trip to the National Pigeon Racing Convention in Blackpool, but again there was no reply at the house. Slightly worried I called Frank, but he'd heard nothing of his old pal throughout the Christmas period. 'If you see him,' said Frank, 'tell him he owes me a score.'

I tried ringing Moonie's house several

more times but there was still no reply, so I started to worry. I got a cab down to the house; there was no sign of life, or at least not human life. As I peered through the window I could see Lou the parrot flapping about in his cage, but there was no sign of Moonie or Gregg. I thought about calling the police or asking his neighbours but I decided against both and instead I walked down to his second home, the Star.

There I asked the barman with the nose like the dried strawberry if he'd seen Moonie. He looked at me suspiciously, so to hurry things along I said I was a friend, a pigeon racing friend. The barman continued to eye me askance until he relented and pointed to a nook and said, 'He's round there.'

Moonie was sat in a corner with Gregg. He didn't look good and Gregg looked sadder than ever. As he saw me walking towards him Moonie gave me a thin smile and raised his glass, slowly stood up and said 'Happy New Year'. I said the same and sat down and after a long pause Moonie filled me in on what had happened over the Christmas holiday.

'I've fucked up,' he slurred.

It quickly became clear that things were not at all well. In fact things, in Moonie's life, had in his own words 'turned to shit' since I'd last seen him.

It had all started not long after our partnership was sealed. Moonie told me that a few nights later there had been more trouble with the neighbours. Moonie had been kept up all night with loud music at a party next door and the day after he had allegedly 'clipped' one of the boys around the head.

From there Moonie had been arrested and then released on a caution after the parents of the boy had eventually dropped the charges of assault. Moonie was thankful that it had gone no further, but during the whole sorry mess the pigeon loft had been broken into and the bulk of his pigeons was now missing.

'Only five or six in there now,' said Moonie with a dreadful sigh of resignation.

I didn't know what to say. I tried to cheer him up as best as I could and said something dumb like 'in the grand scheme of things it's not that bad'. But he looked pretty down and a little defeated.

I felt terrible. I sat with Moonie for a while and tried to lighten the mood, suggesting that with the lost birds being homing pigeons they might come back any minute. He nodded sadly and finished his drink and then I walked him home.

'Don't think I'll be able to spare the birds now,' Moonie said as we approached his house. I told him that wasn't a problem. I would find some more and when I did he could have a share of the winnings just as before. That seemed to buck him up somewhat and as we walked into his house he seemed to have got over the worst of it.

'It's all his fuckin' fault,' Moonie said with a smile on his face, pointing at Lou the parrot. 'If it wasn't for you, me and him would be on our way to a million,' Moonie said, waving his stick at Lou.

Lou didn't say anything. He was flapping around like a mad bird and jumping on and off his perch like his feet were on fire. But he knew when to keep his beak shut. 'More trouble than he's worth,' Moonie said as he walked me to the door. 'Piss up a rope!' I thought I heard Lou squawk, before the door closed behind me.

7

Yul Brynner was a pigeon fancier

'Men may be taught to shoot, fire guns or drill but as Darwin says in the *Origin of the Species* 'It takes years to become a successful pigeon fancier.''

Lt Col. A. H. Osman,
Pigeons and How to Keep Them

I was in the thick of it now. No turning back. I had Frank, Moonie and Lou the parrot depending on me, and behind their masks of beery indifference I could tell they all wanted positive results from the pigeons I hadn't yet purchased.

'I'll be thinking of you over there in South America,' slurred Moonie after an unrequested late-night phone call. 'We'll say a prayer for yer,' he stammered before dropping the phone and hanging up. I presumed the 'we' included his foul-mouthed parrot Lou.

I, of course, wasn't going to South America or South Africa or anywhere just yet. I was still minus the essential ingredients that I

106

needed to enter a pigeon race, i.e. the pigeon, and despite the pleasurable time spent with my new friends, both feathered and otherwise, I continued to be a bit on the 'thick as a bowl of mash' side when it came to the finer points of the art of pigeon flying.

I was several months into my quest now and still lacked the savvy to spot a fledgling from a squab. (A fledgling is a bird that is ready to fly or has just taken its first flight; a squab is a pigeon from one to thirty days old that hasn't left the nest.) What the hell was wrong with me? Barney to Frank's Fred Flintstone; Godber to Les's Fletch; Jim Hawkins to Moonie's Long John Silver. Naive and a little gullible, I was liable to receive the pigeon racing equivalent of the black spot if I didn't get my bumbling act together.

After spending considerable hours delving into the darker recesses of my soul and wondering how I'd arrived at this slightly absurd point, I finally came to the conclusion that it was best not to think about it too much. If I was to get ahead in 'pijin' racing I had to get a grip and know my peepers from my blue bars and my Grooters from my Van Loons.

It was obvious. I needed a good dose of the theory and history of pigeon racing. I needed to acquaint myself with the past masters, the legends. Who was the first man or woman to see the flickering speck appear in a clear blue sky and feel the giddy euphoria in his or her giblets when that feathered wonder came bolting into the loft? I had the practical nous at my disposal — the geniuses residing on various housing estates around Salford and North Manchester — but I had nothing in the way of dust-covered facts and figures.

In an ideal world I wanted to find the Norman Mailer or Ernest Hemingway of pigeon racing. A wise and seasoned scribe to provide weight and substance to the lofty ideas spinning around in my noodle. Like Les had said, it was a science and 'there was more to pigeon racing than cleaning the shit out of the loft.'

With Les on a pre-season buying mission to Holland with the great Gerard Koopman, and Moonie and Frank on a mission to drain the Star of its cheap ales, plus a broken boiler and an ever-decreasing bank balance draining my fragile confidence, I decided to take the opportunity to lock myself indoors and immerse myself in whatever pigeon racing literature I could gather. A recipe for slow encroaching madness it may have been but it was essential nevertheless.

I hoovered up the basics, which were easy enough to find on the many websites serving the pigeon man, woman and child of the world, without too much fuss.

The pigeon on average was around 32 cm in length from bill to tail and weighed less than a pound (0.35 kg). Males were slightly bigger than females. The pigeon was originally descended from the rock dove and one of the earliest records of the dove was to be found thousands of years BC in the story of Noah and the flood. The rock dove was a non-migratory bird that settled into a home for life unless something occurred that would destroy or disrupt that home.

It is more than likely that the Far and Middle Eastern countries were the first to domesticate the rock dove. Over the years the habits and characteristics of the dove evolved, making it eminently suitable for development into a racing pigeon. Ancient records prove that the Japanese bred and used pigeons as messengers. The sultan of Baghdad established a pigeon post system in AD 1150. It is assumed that the racing pigeons of the Western Europeans are descended from those Persian imports known back then as 'Baghdads'. Pigeons were widely used for messenger service in Europe in the 1800s, and for emergency message carriers in war well into the twentieth century. Modern-day pigeon racing, as it is practised today, started in Belgium in the early nineteenth century. The great Mongolian tyrant Ghengis Khan kept pigeons, as did Pablo Picasso, Walt Disney and Frank Zappa. Apparently ruthless Nazi Heinrich Himmler was also a keen pigeon man and was head of the German National Pigeon Association.

The cyber facts were endless but unfortunately, as I slowly discovered, the small library of pigeon literature was limited and more Norman Wisdom than Norman Mailer. Not without a certain charm, but ultimately unrewarding and in parts a bit daft. During a desperate trip to a Lancashire flea market on a dreary wet day I did manage to stumble on an entertaining book called *Pigeon Lore*, written by Major A. Neilson Hutton in 1961.

The book had seen better days and on first glance the prose was a little stodgy. More 'Indigestion in the Morning' than 'Death in the Afternoon'. But as he stared out from the inside of the dusty cover, the major looked like a good old sort, dignified and professional, although possibly with a hint of worry in the weak smile that strained under the perfectly trimmed officer's moustache. He had the slightly uncomfortable countenance of someone who'd forgotten to bolt the pigeon loft and just remembered he'd seen next door's cat nipping round the back gate in the direction of his prized birds.

'The situation, as I see it,' wrote the major in his best Sandhurst prose, 'is that cocks put on to the 'Widowhood System' become stimulated by glandular activities which then bring on peak form.'

Glandular activities? Les had described the Widowhood System method of getting your pigeons to fly faster a little more crudely (but no less clearly) than the major several months previously over a beer.

'The Widowhood System? Basically you get the cock really fuckin' randy. You take the cock to the hen and just when he's thinking about giving her one you take him back to his box. It frustrates the fuck out of 'em and gets them hungry for the race. Just think about it. You'd run a fuckin' mile like Paula Radcliffe if you hadn't had a shag for a few weeks and one was waitin' for yer at the other end, wouldn't yer? Same thing with the pigeons. With the Widowhood System you starve them of sex. The bigger the hard-on the faster they fly.'

The major had been the commander of the Pigeon Service Holding Unit during the Second World War, training pigeons to carry vital messages to and from Algeria and Tunisia. He had been a big fan of pigeons both as a pastime and as an important tool in

111

the push for victory during the war, and he seemed to know his stuff.

'Pigeon racing is a strenuous sport and the path to success, like true love, never runs smooth,' he wrote in conclusion. 'And our few cherished successes are made all the sweeter by our many disappointments.'

Fine sentiments indeed and here was a man who'd seen a thing or two. He'd had more on his plate than the odd debt and a leaky roof in the kitchen (which I'd recently found I now had). The major and his pigeons had taken the fight directly to the Nazis and come out on top. What did I have to complain about? I didn't have to face down Hitler. Just my landlord every now and again, and plough through several dull and musty pigeon books in a cold flat. I didn't know when I was on to a good thing. I repeated that mantra over and over as I read through the books and magazines.

The British pigeon racing fraternity is served by two weekly papers: *British Homing World* and *The Racing Pigeon*. They are both well established trade magazines with a loyal readership of around 20,000. *British Homing World* is the official magazine of the Royal Pigeon Racing Association (the largest pigeon racing organization in the UK) and *The Racing Pigeon* magazine is one of Britain's oldest rags, having been established in 1898.

British Homing World is a forty-nine pence weekly magazine filled with pictures of men in vests holding pigeons; *The Racing Pigeon* is a seventy pence weekly magazine filled with pictures of men in vests holding pigeons.

'You like pigeons?' said the newsagent with a smug grin as I handed over both magazines. 'You never struck me as the type.'

'What's the type?' I said. The boiler still wasn't working, I was washing in the sink and wasn't in the mood to take any guff off the newsagent.

'Flat cap an' all that.'

'There's more to pigeons than flat caps. You don't know the half of it,' I said sharply. I decided to have both the pigeon magazines delivered.

'Cheap and cheerful' is how Frank described the two publications. I couldn't disagree with his analysis as far as the cheap went, but apart from the odd whimsical column title — 'Homer's Odyssey' and 'The Owl and The Pigeon Man' spring to mind — it took me a while to find much of the cheer.

Both magazines were stuffed with racing results and adverts for plywood boxes and pigeon food supplements, with the occasional obituary (recently deceased pigeon racers rather than birds) thrown in, and both were bunged up with the monochrome news and sawdust-tinged views of fanciers from every nook and cranny of this merry isle.

'Inside Sandwell', 'Notes from Bloxwich' and 'Topics from Tivvy' (Tiverton) were among the slices of pigeon life on offer to the keen fancier with a hunger for the minutiae of a week spent in the loft.

Some were adequately written and others not so good, but most of the contributors were pigeon men rather than journalists. That said, like the first time I read Jane Austen, once I grew accustomed to the mores and the manners of the genre the gems soon began to glisten through the mist.

One such gem was a baffling and brilliantly off the wall column in the hallowed pages of *The Racing Pigeon* called Pigeon Talk with 'El Rog'. El Rog was a pigeon racer from Norfolk who had recently upped both sticks and pigeons and moved to Spain. In the black and white photo over his column he looked a little like a balding and bearded Mickey Rooney. He was wearing a dinner suit and he was smiling broadly, like an opulent butcher with a belly full of beer who'd just won a big bottle of whisky in the raffle at a Lion's Club function (which he probably had).

From his Spanish retreat El Rog sent

random thoughts and musings across the pond, most of which had nothing at all to do with pigeons or the racing of them. For example El Rog told the pigeon lovers of Britain about a trip to the bank he had made with his wife, Glenys. One day Rog needed a little money for a 'darts night, a fishing trip and a pack of cigars' but when he and Glenys arrived at the bank they found that the bank had 'no dinero'. Imagine that. A bit of a problem if you want cigars and a darts night, but Rog wasn't the sort of bloke who'd give up his darts and cigars without a struggle. So after a lengthy discussion with the bank teller he got her to scrape together eighty quid from the till so he wouldn't go short of a game of arrows and a good smoke.

Once he'd got the banking incident off his sturdy chest, Rog let us know that he was struggling with the native language. Rog wasn't very good at speaking Spanish, apparently, although he was having regular lessons and trying his best. 'Why aren't I picking this Spanish up as quickly as the others?' said Rog to his exasperated teacher. 'Because you're stupid,' she replied.

I was told by Steve Dunn, the editor of *The Racing Pigeon*, that Michael Shepherd was the closest British pigeon racing had to a seasoned scribe and historian. 'If anyone can help you, Michael can,' said Steve.

Michael had written for *The Racing Pigeon* for over twenty-five years and had flown pigeons for over forty. He lived near Stevenage with his wife Edna and, like all the pigeon men I'd spoken to, he was gracious and more than happy to invite me around for a chat about his passion for the birds. 'You can pop over for a cup of tea,' said Michael in his soft Hertfordshire accent when I rang him up.

Michael was in his late sixties and was a slim and good-humoured man who had dedicated most of his life to pigeons in one way or another. He was now happily semi-retired but for many years he had tended the pigeon loft of the legendary — in pigeon racing circles — Major W. H. Osman.

The major, Michael proudly told me, had been a pigeon man through and through and was the son of Lt Col. A. H. Osman, who, along with the businessman and former MP for Leicester J. W. 'Paddy' Logan, had founded *The Racing Pigeon* magazine in 1898. Logan and Osman were considered to be two of the most important British pigeon racing pioneers, and their names were etched into all the pigeon history books.

'The major got me interested in pigeons,' said Michael as he shuffled over to the dining room table with two mugs of tea. 'I used to live near him and work on his farm and we would have a drink and a chat in the pub. His father the colonel was a great pigeon man. As you may well know, pigeon racing originally started in Belgium in the early nineteenth century, but Paddy Logan and the major were among the founding fathers, if you like, of pigeon racing in this country.'

Michael stood up and left the room before returning with a copy of *The Racing Pigeon*. 'See that pigeon?' said Michael pointing to a picture of a grey checker pigeon under the price box. 'That bird was called Old 86 and it was one of Paddy Logan's most successful birds.' Michael sat back, folded his arms and smiled at the thought of Old 86.

'They both had some very good and very successful pigeons. Like the colonel's pigeon Old Billy, which eventually became the father of the Osman strain of pigeons, the Osman strain being a very sought-after line over the years.'

Michael sipped his tea and thought for a second. 'In some ways, you know, it's a myth that pigeon racing was just a working man's game. Working-class people did race pigeons and keep them, but the pigeon racing you see today in Britain was started by wealthy businessmen like Osman and Logan.'

Michael told me pigeon fancying — keeping birds for aesthetic and intellectual appeal — had been quite common among the wealthier classes from the mid eighteenth century. According to one social commentator of the time, man's growing enjoyment of animals and pets had been born out of the technological advancements of the industrial revolution, which had made the world and nature less inherently threatening. Pigeon fancying had apparently developed out of man's increasing control over nature, plus a wider fashion for bird, butterfly and bee fancying in the early nineteenth century.

'Pigeon racing mainly grew from commerce, from people using pigeons to carry messages in business,' said Michael. 'Different businesses like newspapers and stockbrokers would have a pigeon loft. Not that long ago pigeons would bring in football results for the newspapers and things like that. That's where the expression 'pigeon hole' comes from. The pigeon hole in a newspaper office would more than likely have a pigeon sat in it.'

In the 1840s and '50s the rapid growth of the telegram led to a decline in the use of pigeons for messages, so some of the birds that had been used for messaging were then bought and used for pigeon racing. From there it soon became an integral part of working-class culture, flourishing in the industrial districts of Britain (especially the north of England, South Wales and Central Scotland) in the early part of the twentieth century. At its peak during the 1950s there were over 200,000 pigeon racers in Britain and special 'pigeon express' trains were run each week to transport pigeons to their point of liberation.

'Early on, people in poorer places would keep pigeons to eat and then they began to race them over short distances,' Michael explained. 'Sometimes they would race just a mile down. When people began to make more money they could afford to buy the food and have the lofts that they needed to fly over longer distances, because pigeon racing isn't cheap and never has been. It's always associated with the poorer end of the scale but it has always been a mixture of the working classes and the wealthier people.'

Michael told me that another misconception about pigeon racing was that it wasn't intellectually demanding.

'It's very, very competitive, and breeding is a long and highly skilled process. Feeding and breeding techniques have always been carefully developed over many years and for most good racers they are very closely guarded

119

secrets. It takes a lot of skill and time to work out what you need to have consistently successful pigeons.'

Michael had witnessed such skill at first hand. During his years as a writer and racer he'd struck up a friendship with the late, great Jim Biss, whom some considered, including Michael, to be the best British pigeon racer of his generation.

'Jim was pure gold both as a racer and as a man,' said Michael wistfully. 'And in my mind he is one of the all-time greats.'

Jim Biss had first started racing at the age of ten, having been born into a racing — both pigeon and greyhound — family.

'I suppose racing in one form or another was in his blood,' said Michael, and by way of explanation he told me that Jim's dad had trained greyhounds and at one time had nurtured the great greyhound derby champion of the 1950s, Mick the Miller. That said, Biss senior had, unfortunately, missed out on the dog's glory years.

'Jim's dad bought Mick the Miller from an Irish priest for a lot of money, for a client he had back then. But when the client heard how much he'd paid for the dog he decided he didn't want it, so Jim's dad was left with a big hole in his bank account and Mick the Miller.'

Michael started to laugh as he digressed from the pigeon talk to tell me the tale of Jim Biss's dad and Mick the Miller. 'In those days the rules of greyhound racing were you could not train the dog if you owned it, so the dog's ownership was left in the name of the priest. Anyway, Mick the Miller turned out to be an outstanding dog but he had one weakness. When you put him into a kennel prior to a race he struggled to get out of his coat by chewing the buckles off. So one day he was in the trap and he managed to chew the buckles off, and they found all except one buckle which he'd probably swallowed. Anyway, somebody had been pestering Jim's dad to buy the dog, so he decided that this was the time to sell it, which was unfortunate because he went on to be the greatest greyhound of all time. In fact he was that good he's now stuffed and on display in the Natural History Museum.'

Fortunately for Jim Biss he had a lot more success with the pigeons than his dad had with the greyhounds. Biss won an unprecedented sixteen Nationals in a career that spanned over sixty years.

'Jim was a truly outstanding flyer and perhaps also the greatest all-rounder,' said Michael as he dunked a biscuit into his tea with a flourish. 'You can look at the pioneers and say they were great, but Biss had his success when pigeon racing was established and the competition was much fiercer.'

Jim Biss's pigeons had shown a consistency, and achieved a longevity, that was practically unheard of in pigeon racing.

'I don't like to use the word genius but I think he may have been,' said Michael of his friend.

The other unusual thing about Biss was that he'd bred most of his champions with a strain that dated back to the 1930s. It was a strain that produced a line of pigeons that could fly and be successful at both the shorter and longer distances, which was very difficult to pull off. Biss called his pigeons 'The Great All-Rounders' — they were equally at home sprinting over 200 miles or flying over 700.

'To get a bird to be good at long and short distances is very hard, so Jim's pigeons were very much sought after,' said Michael. 'In fact, when he died we had an auction of his birds and they were sold for a quarter of a million quid. That's how good they were. He was a remarkable man, Jim Biss, and a truly great racer.'

Michael stood up and walked into the kitchen to wash the mugs and I thought he looked a little sad as he reminisced. 'Did you ever meet Frank Zappa? He was a pigeon man apparently,' I shouted to lighten the mood.

'No. But Yul Brynner was a pigeon fancier. Did you know that?'

After nearly choking on what was left of my tea I told Michael I really had no idea.

'Yes he was,' said Michael as he walked back into the front room, looking an awful lot cheerier. 'Yul came over in the early seventies when he was promoting a cowboy film called *Catlow* and his people gave me a call at *The Racing Pigeon*.'

Michael now had a broad smile on his face.

'They called us and said, 'Yul would like to see a pigeon loft,' and so we arranged for him to go and see a loft over in Cockfosters. Actually it was a bit embarrassing. My son Richard was about nine years old at the time and he came with us. Yul and his people were handing out these autographed promotional pictures for the film with Yul in a cowboy outfit. Anyway, they're handing them out at the loft and Yul said to Richard: 'Would you like one of these, son?' And my boy said, 'No. Not particularly.''

Michael laughed excitedly and slapped his leg as he recalled the meeting with one-seventh of the Magnificent Seven. I readied myself to leave.

'You meet some great people in pigeon

racing, you really do, and I think despite all that Yul had a good day at the loft. He wasn't a racer himself though, mind you,' said Michael as he walked me to the front door.

'No?'

'No. He kept fancy pigeons, for show. Like the rollers and the tumblers. Show pigeons. But he was keen and a very pleasant man was Yul Brynner . . . although I didn't realize he was quite so short.'

8

The Homing Odyssey

'What can you conceive more silly and extravagant than to suppose a man racking his brains and studying night and day how to fly?'

William Law,
A Serious Call to a Devout and Holy Life XI (1728)

How does a pigeon find its way home? Surely that's the first question on everyone's lips when racing pigeons are mentioned. How in heavens do those feathered blighters find their way back to the loft from places, often hundreds of miles away, they've never been before? It hadn't escaped my curiosity either. In fact it was the first thing on my mind when I walked into Les's loft. The only problem was the pigeon fancier wasn't the best person to ask. 'Don't have a fuckin' clue,' said Les. 'And to be honest, I don't think anyone does know for sure.'

Les wasn't entirely wrong. The scientists weren't sure but they had been working on the clues.

What scientists call 'true navigation' in pigeons was one of the great mysteries of the ages, like how the Egyptians built the pyramids or who moved the stones to Stonehenge. The navigational sense of birds, and particularly the homing pigeon, has been baffling scientists for centuries, since pigeons were used to carry messages in Ancient Egypt, and Moses was skipping through the reeds in his linen nappy. Even the daddy of Greek philosophers, Socrates, drew a blank when it came to the uncanny homing behaviour of *Columba livia*.

Since Charles Darwin, a pigeon man himself, made the first tentative steps towards explaining the true navigation phenomenon in 1873 — he thought the birds had an ability to register all the twists and turns of the outward journey and remember them for the way back — science has tried, and mostly failed, to get to grips with the mechanisms that underlie the remarkable ability of homing pigeons to navigate to and from unfamiliar sites.

There have been several theories as to why pigeons home, some stronger than others, but three very different theories prevail today.

During the 1950s, the golden years of pigeon racing when around 500,000 fanciers roamed the British Isles and the pigeon was considered a war hero after its many daring missions to enemy territory, a scientist called G. V. T. Matthews proposed that pigeons used the 'arc of the sun' to home back to the loft. They could determine direction and position using only information provided by the sun. The pigeon, he reckoned, had an internal clock and map, and by combining the position of the sun and its movement in the sky the pigeon could work out how to get home. It was a logical enough proposal, if you studied that type of thing, but this theory was soon dismissed due to the pigeon's uncanny knack of returning on a cloudy day, or at night.

William Keeton at Cornell University in New York, however, did not dismiss the sun as navigation tool completely out of hand. Keeton reasoned that, because of its ability to home on overcast days, the bird must be using another system in addition to the sun compass. He thought that the sun was used to obtain directional information when it was visible, but that pigeons must have some kind of secondary compass sense that enabled them to navigate home when the sun was nowhere to be seen. He concluded that that second sense could be an ability to detect the earth's magnetic field and use it to navigate like a compass. It was known as magnetic cue theory.

To try and prove this theory that the pigeon had an inbuilt map and compass, Keeton released a batch of pigeons on a cloudy day in 1971 and waited for them to home to the loft, some with bar magnets glued to their bodies and some with brass bars attached to their heads and backs. What Keeton found was that five out of six of the pigeons without magnets returned successfully but the pigeons with magnets attached were, according to a report by Cornell University, 'either random or not homeward oriented'. It looked pretty good for Keeton's magnetic cue theory. Had the mystery of true navigation finally been cracked? Well, not exactly. After further experiments Keeton found that most of the pigeons with magnets attached, after the initial disorientation, would home successfully on an overcast day, and when the sun was out they had fewer problems getting home. Magnetism wasn't dismissed out of hand, however, and several other theories based on pigeons responding to subtle variations in the earth's magnetic fields were and still are cited as the reason pigeons can navigate home.

Another popular theory of the 1970s that gradually replaced the magnetism idea came from Italy and dealt with the pigeon's ability to smell its way home.

The University of Pisa has had a history of radical scientific theories since the seventeenth century, when Galileo theorized that the earth orbited the sun. Floriano Papi's theory that pigeons couldn't home without the sense of smell wasn't quite as groundbreaking as Galileo's, but it wasn't that far off in terms of animal behaviour. Papi's research found that pigeons created odour maps of their neighbourhoods — an olfactory map — and could use these to orient themselves by associating the odours with the direction of the wind. For example in Manchester a pigeon wanting to fly to the north side of town would head towards the unmistakable hoppy whiff of the Boddingtons brewery.

The Italian smell theory was known as the factory hypothesis and was given extreme credence when it became apparent that birds whose nasal membrane had been anaesthetized could not home successfully.

In 2004 the factory theory was backed up still further when an experiment by Anna Gagliardo of the University of Pisa — smell theorist — and Martin Wild of the University of Auckland — magnetic theorist — went head to head.

To prove which theory was the strongest

Wild cut the nerves that carried olfactory signals in twenty-four young homing pigeons and in another twenty-four he cut the trigeminal nerve, which is linked to the part of the brain involved in detecting magnetic fields.

The forty-eight birds were released thirty miles from their loft and after twenty-four hours all but one of the birds deprived of the ability to detect magnetic fields were home. The pigeons whose ability to smell had been taken flew over the skies of Italy in disarray. Only four made it home.

'This is important because it is the first time that magnetic sensing and smell have been tested side by side,' Gagliardo told the *Daily Telegraph*.

However, other theories still remained. 'Evidence of factory theory is convincing but it is not the only theory,' said Professor Tim Guilford, reader in animal behaviour at Oxford University's Department of Zoology.

Guilford and his team had been working for years on the idea that pigeons used visual cues to navigate back to the loft, following landmarks and main roads — what he also referred to as steeplechasing.

Visual cues received little attention, compared to olfactory and magnetic theories, probably due to an experiment by William

Keeton in 1974 where pigeons equipped with frosted lenses still managed to make it home. Neverthless Guilford and his distinguished colleagues at Oxford still made strong claims in favour of visual cues.

Guilford's team carried out dozens of tests using small GPS tracking devices stuck to the back of each pigeon. The pigeons were released twenty or thirty miles from home and on return the data on the GPS, which had recorded the exact flight paths of the pigeons, was logged into a computer. What Guilford and his team found was that the pigeons often 'followed their own individual habitual routes home and not often the most direct, so it (the homing instinct) is more than energetic efficiency.' In other words, Guilford thought the pigeon was less likely to fly as the crow flies and more likely to follow the A34 Oxford bypass.

It was an interesting theory and one that could certainly explain the movement of birds over familiar landscapes, but this did not explain the process by which birds find their way home from places they've never been before. 'That still remains a mystery,' said Guilford.

There was one man who thought he might be on a more unconventional path to solving that mystery, however. Rupert Sheldrake PhD was the former director of studies in biochemistry at Clare College, Cambridge University, and the author of *The Rebirth of Nature*, *A New Science of Life* and *Dogs That Know When They Are Coming Home*.

Sheldrake challenged conventional scientific theories around many subjects including the true navigation of the pigeon. He said, 'There has been a whole range of theories but the evidence against them is stronger than the evidence for.'

Sheldrake wanted to challenge what he called the 'scientific priesthood'. He wanted to find other ways to explain the unexplained and he wasn't afraid to peer into the murky hole of what many would refer to as the paranormal.

In his book *Seven Experiments That Could Change the World*, Sheldrake wrote:

institutional science has become so conservative, so limited by the conventional paradigms, some of the most fundamental problems are either ignored, treated as taboo, or put at the bottom of the scientific agenda . . . For example, the direction-finding abilities of migratory and homing animals, such as monarch butterflies and homing pigeons, are very mysterious. They have not been explained in terms of orthodox science, and perhaps they cannot be.

Sheldrake had a theory that, rather than smells or main roads, pigeons found their way home by way of the theory of morphic resonance. Everyone agrees that pigeons can use familiar features, such as roads, when they are near home, but that they cannot use landmarks as a way of finding their way back from distant, unfamiliar places. Sheldrake proposes that they use a 'sense of direction' that depends on a 'morphic field . . . something rather like an invisible elastic band connecting them to their home and drawing them back towards it'. They may also use clues from smell, when near home, or a magnetic compass sense to keep them on course, but this field sense is the most important component of their navigation system when they are in unfamiliar terrain.

Sheldrake was confident about his theory and, on hearing about his quirky and unconventional ideas, a British independent television company, Ikon Films, contacted him and invited him to appear on a Channel 5 programme that hoped to explain the mysterious homing instinct of the pigeon.

Sheldrake agreed and set up a radical new experiment, never before seen on TV, that he hoped would have the morphic resonance-sceptical scientists laughing on the other side of their beaks.

Pigeons were usually taken to a place they'd never been before and asked to return home. Sheldrake planned to take them to an unfamiliar spot and ask them to home to a loft that had been removed and placed in a spot they'd also never been before. It was ambitious, and the first TV and pigeon true-navigation experiment of its kind.

It was, for want of a better name, the floating loft experiment.

In 2005 Sheldrake, using twenty-two fledgling pigeons owned by a fancier called Raggsy, set up a loft on a pontoon on the River Severn. Over several months the pigeons called it home and were more than happy there until one day Sheldrake moved the loft a hundred yards down the river.

This was the first part of the experiment. Would the pigeons work out that the loft had been shifted down-stream? After several hours of flying around the empty spot where the loft used to be, the answer to that question was yes, the pigeons found the new location of the loft, albeit a short flap downriver, and all was still well with the morphic resonance theory. But this was only the first tiny step.

The real test came when the birds were taken and released while the loft and Raggsy were loaded onto a sand dredger and floated onto open water forty or so miles downstream on the Severn estuary.

It was a bold move but one that had to be done if the pull of the 'invisible elastic band' was to be heard twanging loudly around the corridors of Oxford, Cambridge, Pisa and beyond.

Was morphic resonance, the attachment to the loft and the owner, the key to unlocking the great mystery of true navigation in pigeons? Were Sheldrake's seemingly flakey and unconventional ideas actually grounded in the firm concrete of hard evidence? Well, in terms of the floating loft experiment, no.

After twenty-four hours not a single pigeon had found the loft out in the open water and not long after that, the TV and boat crew, wanting to get in out of the cold, I imagine, saw fit to abort the mission. Sheldrake's unconventional theory had taken something of a body blow. Oxford, Cornell and Pisa Universities could breathe a sigh of relief and could possibly revel in a victory for more conventional scientific methods. But the victory was a hollow one. The mystery of true navigation remained as elusive as ever, and maybe Les wasn't far off the mark after all. When it came to the homing instinct of the pigeon, it certainly looked as though we 'didn't have a fuckin' clue'.

9

Bollocks to the dead parrot!

Take these broken wings
And learn to fly again
Learn to live so free

Mr Mister,
'Broken Wings'

'Hey, Buddy Holly, would you like some black pudding?' said Pat.

I was back at Les's loft in Oldham and Pat was frying some black pudding on the small stove. He called me Buddy Holly because I wore dark-framed glasses. I guess he couldn't think of anybody else who wore dark-framed glasses after 1960.

'No thanks, Pat.'

'What about some cheese? Would you like some cheese? I've got some good old Irish cheese here.'

Pat was a pigeon man from Dublin and an esteemed friend and colleague of Les and the Wall, Lunt, Galley and Green pigeon team. He had left Ireland many moons before but his addiction to all things feathered had followed him to Manchester and he carried out odd jobs for Les and the gang around the loft — knocking together plywood pigeon boxes, among other things — and at the pigeon sales — Pat was one of the baggy-trousered duo who'd boxed up the pigeons at the Koopman sale in Irlam.

'I get this shipped over special from Ireland,' said Pat with an avaricious grin, while proudly holding up a blue plastic carrier bag full of black pudding, cheese and cream crackers as though it were a sack of Spanish gold.

'Can't you buy black pudding and cheese and crackers over here?' I enquired somewhat naively.

'Can yer fuck. Not this sort. Do you want some cheese or what?'

'No thanks, Pat.'

'What's wrong with yer?' Suddenly Pat looked horrified. He screwed up his face and gave me a look as though I'd morphed into Saddam Hussein, grabbed one of his pigeons and was holding it by the throat. In fact Pat's look said 'Not only are you Saddam and you have my pigeon by the throat and you are grinning but you have the brass-faced cheek to turn down my black pudding and cheese.'

'Good Irish grub this is,' he said, scratching

his head under his old woollen hat and then, with the same hand, pulling a cream cracker from the packet and spreading a thick slab of butter over it until it crumbled and broke like a Dead Sea scroll.

I was at the loft for a summit meeting of sorts. Crisis talks, if you like. Recent events, out of our control, were threatening to turn the pigeon racing world upside down and we feared that things were about to turn ugly. An attack on the pigeon was imminent, and we were all bracing ourselves.

'What about some ham?' asked Pat. 'I've got a nice bit of ham here.'

'No thanks, Pat.'

'Ahh, suit yer fuckin' self.'

It had all started with a parrot, or to be precise a dead parrot, or to be even more accurate a consignment of parrots with a dead parrot on board that had arrived on these shores from Surinam in South America in September 2005. They had been quarantined in Essex while investigations into the death of the dead parrot were carried out.

The dead parrot was suspected of carrying bird flu, or, to give its other slightly grander name, avian influenza (AI). Soon the parrots, dead and otherwise, weren't alone. Ten days after they were banged up in quarantine, the parrots were joined in bird chokey by a group of mesia birds — a breed of finch — who arrived in a mixed consignment of birds from Taiwan.

While in quarantine some of the finches, like the parrot, croaked, and all the birds were then suspected and tested for avian influenza — in particular for the deadly H5N1 strain of the virus which had allegedly been responsible for the hundred or so human deaths worldwide.

At the beginning of the dead parrot saga, like most fairly normal people I was frustrated by the lack of common sense being applied to the reporting of the subject in the British press. Even in the countries — mainly in East Asia — where the H5N1 strain had spread to a level that could be considered 'an outbreak', the threat to humans was minimal. Although each death was a terrible tragedy, by the end of 2005 the World Health Organization had reported around one hundred deaths linked to bird flu. Nevertheless 'Outbreak Imminent!' was the general gist of the headlines in the red tops and confusion and panic began to seep into the fragile psyche of the nation.

Like the never-to-materialize SARS outbreak that was promised a few years before, the discovery of the dead parrot provoked a wave of fear and all things feathered were eyed suspiciously, like the enemy within. It was a reaction something akin to the simple folk of America's backwaters in the 1940s running for their pitchforks and bloodhounds after tuning in to Orson Welles's radio broadcast of *The War of The Worlds*.

I wasn't alone in my frustration at the panic when it came to the speculation surrounding an outbreak. 'Bird flu is fast turning our feathered friends into feathered fiends,' wrote Tony Juniper in the *Guardian* under the headline 'Less hype, more knowledge is needed to tackle bird flu'.

'If we are to believe the reports, anything with a beak is becoming something to be feared,' Juniper fumed and he, apparently, knew a thing or two about our feathered friends. He had penned a book with the intriguing title *Spix's Macaw* and co-authored another rather more simply entitled tome called *Parrots*.

'The parrot that died has become an icon of menace. But no one seemed to care what kind it was. There were TV pictures of all kinds of parrots — conures, macaws and amazons included. One report even showed an owl,' Juniper complained.

The parrot under scrutiny, for the record, had been of the blue-headed variety but no matter. I binned the papers, turned off the telly and trawled the more reliable scientific

141

press for a few facts and figures that would throw some light on the whole sorry saga.

Domestic fowl, ducks, geese, turkey, guinea fowl, quail and pheasants were most susceptible to the virus according to a report by the FAO (Food and Agricultural Organization of the United Nations). Of the wild bird species water birds and seabirds were also susceptible to infection, although the strain that tended to circulate in wild birds was of the low pathogenic variety, i.e. non-deadly. The disease, though, was generally thought to have spread through contact between these wild birds and domestic poultry, where, said the FAO, 'a virulent strain may emerge either by genetic mutation or by reassortment of less virulent strains.'

Still no word about pigeons but I read on. A leading expert on AI called Pat Thomas, writing in the *Ecologist* magazine, said there were 'sixteen types of bird flu and of the sixteen known types three subtypes — H5, H7 & H9 — are known to be capable of crossing the species barrier'.

The upshot of the panic surrounding bird flu was the possibility of the disease mutating to a form that could be carried and passed on from human to human but the seemingly rational Pat Thomas didn't seem to be unduly worried at the prospect of this AI mutation.

'Even if the virus were to jump species,' he wrote 'it may not necessarily spread through the human population as it has with chickens. Since 1997 types H5N1, H7N2, H7N3, H7N7, and H9N2 have all caused small, confirmed outbreaks in humans throughout the world. The fact that a virus can cross the species barrier, however, does not mean that it is dangerous. For instance, just because H5N1 is lethal in chickens doesn't necessarily mean that it will be so in humans.'

Thomas went on to reassure us, or me at least, that since the 2002 outbreak of H5N1 there had been billions of interactions between chickens and humans yet the number of humans worldwide who had been infected with the disease had been extremely low. From 2002 to 2004 there were only 118 and these cases were largely confined to Vietnam, Cambodia and Thailand. The most serious epidemics occurred in Hong Kong in 1997–98 and 2003, The Netherlands in 2003 and South Korea in 2003.

On 21 October 2005, it was reported that the H5N1 strain had finally been confirmed in one of the parrots under quarantine in Essex. Fortunately, because the bird was in quarantine, this did not affect the disease-free status of the UK. However, DEFRA (Department for Environment, Food and Rural

143

Affairs), fearing another foot and mouth type crisis, thought it prudent to take precautions in case of an outbreak.

Preparations for a mass cull of the nation's poultry were put in place and Ruttle Plant Hire in Chorley, who were the fourth-biggest contractor used to dig disposal pits for slaughtered, sheep, pigs and cattle during the foot and mouth crisis, were contacted by DEFRA and placed on standby. 'As yet they haven't decided whether to bury or burn the carcasses, but what is clear is that any cull of poultry would be easier than cattle.' Arthur Ruttle, the Ruttle Plant Hire company director, told the press that the nation could rest easy. Or could it?

By the end of October 2005 it was reported that the virus had spread across Russia, through Turkey — where a young girl's death was linked to her close contact with an infected chicken — and into Croatia. German vets were carrying out tests on thirty-five dead wild geese and ducks. A month later and the story in the UK suddenly turned once again. After further tests the blue-headed parrot was out of the frame and the Taiwanese mesia birds — the finches — were well and truly in it.

'On the balance of probabilities,' said the National Emergency Epidemiology Group, the disease was more likely to have come from the finches than the parrot.

The Conservative party were quick to beat the government with the dead parrot and the dead finch. 'This is yet another worrying indication that confusion reigns,' said Conservative environment spokesman Oliver Letwin. You could say that again. Confusion did indeed reign and no one, it seemed, was safe.

Even the filthy rich and their birds were under threat. Abramovich — Roman not Koopman — didn't escape the panic and neither did his parrot. As the bird flu fears gathered pace it was revealed that the billionaire Chelsea owner's African grey parrot who lived, unlike the East Asian battery hens, in obscene luxury on board a £60 million cruiser yacht called *Le Grand Bleu*, was also under threat of seizure and quarantine. In mid November 2005 the African grey was on its way to New Zealand — for a well-earned break — but the holiday was ruined when the Kiwi authorities began to squawk 'bird flu', and the billionaire's exotic feathered mucker was impounded.

'Mr Abramovich, who is estimated to be worth more than £7.5 bn, will have to foot the bill for a series of tests on the bird which is dubbed the 'Cadillac of parrots' thanks to its gift of speech,' wrote Bernard O'Riordan in the *Guardian*.

All this chaos begged the question: if the parrot of a Russian billionaire oligarch wasn't safe, what about the pigeon loft of an honest working man like Les Green?

'It's all fuckin' bollocks,' said Les as he burst into the cabin, nearly knocking over Pat's plate of black pudding.

'Bollocks to the dead parrot. This is typical scaremongering. I've heard all this stuff before,' he sneered.

'All fuckin' nonsense it is,' Pat chipped in usefully between mouthfuls.

Whether it was nonsense or not the threat of a bird flu outbreak was about to seriously disrupt, and in the worst case postpone, the 2006 racing season. DEFRA had categorized the pigeon as low risk, but there were still significant problems ahead.

In October 2005 the European Union made its first step towards preventing the spread of AI by imposing a ban on bird gatherings, shows, fairs and any other similar events. It was, in Les's eyes, a minor inconvenience but it meant that pigeon sales such as the Koopman sale, where birds were shipped from abroad, were under threat, and if an outbreak did take place it was likely that birds of any kind would be prevented from

146

moving wherever possible.

This was the harsh reality that the average and not so average pigeon man was waking up to, and the rumours were flying around like, erm, worried pigeons. Would the RPRA be issuing rings in 2006? Would pigeons be able to fly from France? Was the *BHW (British Homing World)* Show of the Year at Blackpool definitely on? These were some of the hot questions on the lips of the nation's racing fraternity.

'Unbelievable it is,' said Les, steadying himself on the draining board and prodding what was left of the black pudding in the frying pan with disdain. 'In fact it's not unbelievable, it's very fuckin' believable,' he continued, before rolling up a copy of the *Daily Star* and beginning to wave it around like a mildly deranged symphony conductor.

'There's one of these panics at least once a year. Salmonella, SARS, Mad fuckin' cow disease!' he roared, stomping around the cabin, his voice suddenly rising: 'Mad cow disease! We were all supposed to be monged out on that by now,' His voice had now reached the level of a macaw-like screech.

'The biggest panic of the lot that fuckin' was and you never even hear a peep about it now. The French stopping our meat goin' over there an' all that. Load of shite. And now it's the same again. All this bollocks about bird flu.'

Les sat down and slugged a mouthful of Pat's tea and tried to reason it through. 'We all know it's not about the birds gettin' the flu. It's about the bastard thing mutating. Which is a load of old fanny. If it mutates into humans and then humans pass it on to humans, then it will wipe a load of us out. That's what it's all about but that's a load of shite. We've got more chance of getting wiped out by a fuckin' big asteroid than by a parrot.'

'It wasn't the parrot, it was a finch,' I boldly interjected.

Les rose from his seat and thrust the rolled-up copy of the *Daily Star* in my direction.

'People in Third World countries who live with chickens in the fuckin' house and sleep with the bastards, that's who get it and only seven of them fuckers 'ave died. So what's the chance of us fuckin' dyin'? That kid who died in Turkey she was nursing the dying chickens. Fuckin' cuddlin' 'em. Fuckin' 'ell, and the other poor fuckers who died were eating the fuckin' things. Eatin' the infected chickens! It's small wonder they died, innit!'

Les clearly felt very strongly about the subject and his face turned a similar purple to the bottle of fizzy Vimto that was cooling in a

148

bucket full of water under the TV. Also, for good measure, he'd suddenly turned into Salford's answer to Alf Garnett.

'It's another way for the authorities to have a go at the fuckin' pigeon racer. That's what it is an' all. It's an excuse to fuck us over. They've got us — the racing pigeon — in the same category as the street pigeon. Wild birds, they've said. How can you call racing pigeons wild birds? Unbelievable. That's how much they know about what we do. They know fuck all.'

Les's face had now cooled to a bright crimson but he wasn't quite finished.

'And the other thing is there's no evidence to say that pigeons are prone to bird flu. None whatsoever.'

'But they're birds so surely they have a chance of picking it up?' I stupidly offered.

'Well of course they're fuckin' birds, Columbo. But some birds are more inclined to get it than others. If you look at the birds that 'ave got it it's mainly chickens. Poultry an' that. That you keep cooped up in stinking places that nobody cleans. Battery chickens 'an that. They pick it up off birds that are eating and drinking out of the same place and breathing the same air. Pigeons aren't totally immune to it but they have a strong immune system and they're certainly right down on the list when it comes to any chance of getting it.'

Les was unequivocal. Racing pigeons weren't a threat to humanity and they would not bring an end to civilization as we knew it. He had made it clear where he stood but despite his vociferous claims the threat to the 2006 pigeon racing season was a real one, and the nervous rumblings in the racing fraternity were clearly audible, even in Moonie's far-flung outpost.

'We'll be lucky if we get any racing at all this year,' said Moonie somewhat cheerily, as he doused his loft down with disinfectant several days after my meeting with Les. 'Stan the 'oracle' says that the pigeon rings won't be issued by the RPRA and he says there'll be no flying from France.'

Stan 'the oracle' was the landlord at the Star and a self-proclaimed expert on everything from the siege of Stalingrad to the life and times of George Formby but, despite Moonie's insistence that 'Stan was the man when it came to pigeons', I doubted it. The 'oracle's considerable knowledge and expertise stretched far and wide but not, I sensed, to the world of pigeon racing and its current precarious state.

The whole issue, and especially Moonie, had put me on a downer. I needed some reassurance that my dream of pigeon-racing glory wouldn't be dashed before I'd even left my pit. A more reliable view than the pub landlord was possibly in order. Someone who knew what the dickens he was talking about — and that man was Peter Bryant.

Peter Bryant was an ex-RAF administrator who now held the title of general manager of the RPRA — the biggest and most prestigious pigeon racing association in the UK, with 36,000 members — although, strangely, he'd never flown a pigeon in his life. But he didn't let that hold him back. 'I didn't fly an aeroplane but that didn't stop me doing my job as an administrator with the RAF,' Peter always said.

Peter was the equivalent of the Head of the FA, the public face of pigeons in the UK. He'd been on radio and TV championing the cause of the pigeon, was in the thick of it when it came to PR and promotions and was the man on the front line when it came to fighting fires of the pigeon-related kind.

Contrary to some beliefs, Peter's job wasn't easy. Keeping the nation's pigeon fanciers — it had more than its share of curmudgeons and complainers — content was no picnic. But Peter took the rough with the smooth and showed a serviceman's stoicism, especially during the bird flu crisis of 2005.

I rang Peter at the RPRA office in Cheltenham for some reassurance that I still had a chance to compete in the 'big one'.

'I can assure you there will be racing this year,' said Peter in his reedy West Country accent.

Thank the gods for that.

'There have been some stupid rumours doing the rounds but I can assure you that the rings for 2006 have been sent out and DEFRA have said that racing can take place this year.'

Marvellous news, Peter.

'We got the clearance just before Christmas but it does restrict us at the moment to racing within the UK, excluding the Channel Islands, and of course there are bio-security measures that we have to undertake which are not onerous.'

Bio-security measures? This sounded quite serious but Peter sounded pretty relaxed about it all.

'They are things we have to do as a matter of course and in fact it exceeds what is required. We were pretty clued up so the only restriction is that we have to race within the UK.'

All in all it sounded like positive news. But something still worried me. If birds could not race outside of the UK how would that affect birds being transported out of the country? How could we send birds to South Africa if our movements were restricted to the UK?

'Well that's a different ball game altogether,' said Peter ominously.

I held my breath.

'That really comes under the import and export of livestock and different countries have got different agreements. One of the weekly round robins — almost daily round robins — we get from DEFRA are restrictions placed on British birds and livestock. For example there are a lot of countries in the Middle and Far East who will not accept poultry at the moment, for obvious reasons. Some European countries have put temporary bans on. We traditionally send out pigeons to a race in Mira, Portugal and they actually stopped us sending birds out there this year, but as far as I'm aware there have been no restrictions on racing pigeons going to South Africa. Despite the fact that pigeons have great resistance to avian flu there's still an if or but about it.'

South Africa was still on. I took some grains of solace from that. Bird flu panic had gripped the nation but the authorities had had the good sense not to go overboard and come down too hard on the humble racing pigeon. Thanks to Peter and the RPRA a small victory had been won for the little man, and his pigeons. Things were looking up once again. I could concentrate on the important issues in my life like purchasing a winning breed of pigeon for the big race. Not only that, I could look forward to the upcoming extravaganza that was the National Pigeon Racing Convention in Blackpool. The annual gathering of the country's finest pigeon men was just around the corner.

'You're in with me and Pat and the boys,' said Les when I rang him with the good news I'd got from Bryant. 'All booked up. It's fuckin' great. You'll never see as many bad outfits in your life.'

Blackpool in late January. The nation's best pigeon racers. All booked but still to be paid for. Surely life doesn't get much better than that.

10

Bittersweet Blackpool

Turn it up, turn it up loud,
Turn it up loud for the Blackpool crowd.

> Sham 69, 'Blackpool'

Les had warned me it was going to be messy. '25,000 pigeon men take over Blackpool,' he said, making it sound like a 1950s sci-fi B movie starring Arthur Askey. 'So get a good scran down yer neck. A good lining on your stomach . . . essential that is.' I bet they didn't say that to George Clooney before the Oscars.

The National Pigeon Racing Convention in Blackpool was that sort of weekend, though. It was the biggest single gathering of pigeon racing men and women in Europe and (if they had a few strands left) they liked to let their hair down. Les hadn't missed many of these events since the Convention was moved from Doncaster in 1977 due to the huge numbers of attendees and the consequent need for a bigger and more glamorous venue

155

— back in 1977 Blackpool had what Doncaster lacked: fun, sea and Freddie Starr on the South Pier. You had to go a long way to beat Blackpool back then.

Anyway, Les loved it. All pigeon men did. For one weekend every year at the back end of January it was pigeon paradise in the Vegas of the north. There were pigeon sales, pigeon stalls and pigeon shows — the *British Homing World* Show of the Year in the Winter Gardens — and pigeon gala dinners. More importantly, for the great majority of those thirsty pigeon men and women, there was plenty of pigeon chat in late-night hotel bars, as well as what seemed like a never-ending supply of booze.

'They like a drink, the pigeon lads,' Les had hugely understated some weeks before the event. 'They like a pint. But on the whole they behave themselves. It's all good fun. It's a bit like Hallowe'en. You've never seen as many scary fuckers and as many bad outfits in your life as you do at Blackpool. Fat old blokes with green leather jackets and piano ties tryin' it on with young birds an' all that. It's fuckin' great.'

'Sold!' I told Les.

The convention was a time and a place for the average British fancier to unwind, to drink and talk pigeons, and then drink and talk pigeons some more. You could sample the delights of Blackpool in mid winter, scoff rock and chocolate cocks and whatever culinary delights and local smutty confectionery you fancied, before finally staggering up the musty stairwell of a drafty Blackpool B&B and spewing over your newly acquired pigeon worth £5,000. The convention was the highlight of the British pigeon racing calendar — Crufts, the G8 summit and the Oscars rolled into one huge pigeon-fuelled piss-up — and I was looking forward to it. Enormously.

Like Les I was a fan of Blackpool. Or at least I liked the idea of what I thought Blackpool had been in the seventies and the early eighties, my age of innocence, when I'd holidayed there and didn't know better. Blackpool had been a staple of my childhood, like corned beef fritters and Tizer. It had been the family holiday destination of choice. It was convenient, unpretentious and affordable.

The long, warm coach rides, and the slightly sickly giddy feeling in my stomach as I anticipated the first sighting of the Tower in the distance, were as glowingly remembered as warm nights watching the 1982 World Cup and jumping home-made ramps in the churchyard on my Grifter. Cherished memories. Even the Blackpool stag dos of my late teens had a certain warm, hazy and comforting resonance, and the miserable landladies, dishing out stale kippers and soggy cornflakes in guest houses that had all the charm of a Chubby Brown mother-in-law tirade, lived on fondly in my noodle.

The yin and yang of Blackpool sat comfortably together in my psyche. Those wonderful opposites nestled snuggly. Mirth and Misery strolled along the prom, hand in sticky hand. The fun was always followed by a knee-grazing fall. It was part of the Blackpool experience. One man's beer-filled delight was always another man's head over the toilet, retching into the night. Bittersweet Blackpool. The first Gulf war had been raging the last time I'd smelt the sweet Irish Sea air mixed with candy floss and chips. The Scuds had been flying and Saddam's elite Republican Guard had been fleeing as I'd shimmied around the Tower ballroom dance floor to the wonky warblings of a third-rate Gloria Estefan soundalike accompanied by a gaggle of women from the psychiatric hospital and the local chicken factory.

'Have you got room in the van?' I said.

'Yeah, on the fuckin' roof,' said Les.

★ ★ ★

It was ten o'clock on the morning of the convention and a wind marginally warmer than the one Captain Oates had walked bravely into that fateful day in the Antarctic was whistling around Les's pigeon loft at the back of his house in Irlam.

Les and Ray had been busy all morning counting and boxing up pigeons for the sale that evening. Les was in the loft calling out the numbers on the elastic ring around the leg of each pigeon and Ray was ticking the numbers off on a clipboard and placing each pigeon in a cardboard Amtrak box. The pigeons had been sent to Les by various breeders for the sale in Blackpool, the sale that Les had billed as 'The Night of the Stars'.

'Who are the stars?' I asked Les. 'The pigeons?'

'No, not the fuckin' pigeons,' Les shouted from the loft. 'Some of the biggest stars in the game, that's all.'

The 'stars' in question, as well as Les and the boys, were the ubiquitous Gerard Koopman and several other big-name Belgian and Dutch pigeon racers who weren't going to be there but had shipped over their pigeons — regardless of the bird flu scare — for the star-studded sale that would take place in the ballroom of the Savoy hotel in Blackpool.

The stars weren't going to make it and it was even touch and go if Koopman would turn up, but Les expected a big turn-out and a nice earner to boot. 'These are the highest-quality birds,' he said. 'It doesn't get any better than these.'

Les had around 160 pigeons from the stars of European pigeon racing and he was taking his usual cut of around 20 per cent. The previous year his sales had bagged him around £40,000. Blackpool had been good to Les.

'I think we've got some missing here, Les,' said Ray from under his woolly hat. 'I think it's fucked up.'

Ray looked puzzled. The numbers on his clipboard didn't correspond with the numbers on the pigeons. Les came to investigate, looking less than impressed and his face a little blue from the cold. Les and Ray had been doing this for the past three hours. Checking and boxing. It was an essential part of the pigeon sale as it tended to help the sale if you knew which birds were which.

'1518910,' said Ray pointing out the number on the clipboard, 'that isn't there. And 911. That isn't there either.'

'911, he's a good one. Goes like a fuckin' bomb. But don't fly him near tall buildings,' Les joked as he grabbed the clipboard and pulled a face.

160

'Ray, you are a blind speccy bastard. I remember that being there. It had a little frill on its neck. There he is, I can see him from here. Fuckin' useless you are.'

'It happens when you get old, you know,' said Ray as Les marched back to the loft to finish off the sales check. 'I fuckin' hate doin' this,' he continued. 'This is the bit I hate most. You have to do this when you go racing. Put them in the basket and put the numbers on them and check them off. I hate that part of it.'

'The quicker the people that run pigeon racing latch on to what we should be doing, all this marking up pigeons with a biro will be forgotton and we can move on with the business of flying the fuckin' things!' Les shouted from the loft.

What do they have to latch on to?

'Simple. Electronic tagging,' said Ray. 'Then you don't have to do this. The Dutch and the Belgians have electronic tags on their pigeons. Everybody does. Even the Jocks are on it. It's just us lot. They are hypocritical at the RPRA. They have a one-loft race every year and they use the ETS — that's the Electronic Timing System to you — for that but they won't let us use it here.'

I asked why not and said I presumed the Blackpool convention would be the sort of place where you could have debates about that kind of thing. I thought pigeon problems would be ironed out with round-table discussions in between trips to the bar.

'We've had loads of debates about it,' said Les, stepping out of the loft, pigeon in hand. 'There'll be a stand there at Blackpool bigger than this loft promoting the ETS system, but nobody is using it.'

There was no such thing as democracy in pigeon racing according to Les and Ray. No chance for pigeon club members to vote on burning issues such as ETS. Pigeon men, so Ray and Les told me, worked within a dictatorship. Albeit a mild-mannered one that usually worked and did the best for its people, often against tremendous odds. Pigeon racing was like Cuba under Castro.

'Peter Bryant [General Manager of the RPRA] is OK. He does what he has to do and he's a good administrator, but he's not a pigeon man. He doesn't want to rock the boat,' said Les. 'And the system democratic? You must be joking,' he scoffed.

'Put it this way, me and Gary went to Utrecht a few years ago. 1995, I think it was, and the main guy from the RPRA back then, Major Camilleri, was on the boat with us. We mentioned introducing the ETS system to the UK and he said, 'Oh no, we don't want

162

that over here in the UK, that will be the end of all of us.' That's their attitude.'

The introduction of the Electronic Timing System was a debate that raged in lofts up and down the country, but the majority of pigeon racers I'd spoken to were in favour of it. Unfortunately the RPRA and the editors of its official paper — *British Homing World* — were not; even they thought they were delaying the inevitable, however. You couldn't halt progress, not even in pigeon racing.

'ETS is very divisive,' said a spokeswoman at *Homing World* when I called to ask about the pros and cons of the system. 'Some fanciers feel it gives them a lot of freedom as pigeon racing currently demands your personal attendance on race day. ETS clocks-in the birds automatically as they pass over a sensor pad which auto-records their time. The disability discrimination act requires that the sport allows electronic timing for disabled fanciers, so, love it or hate it, it seems that ETS is not an option and we ignore it at our peril.'

Those in favour of ETS argued it was less stressful for the pigeon, as you didn't have to handle it on its return to the loft on race day, and it was also less stress for the pigeon man, especially the ageing and ailing one. ETS was of benefit to the older racers whose hands and footing weren't as steady as they used to be. Those against the electronic system argued about the expense of setting it up — if ETS was to work all fanciers would have to upgrade to the computerized system — and some said it gave the top racers, like Les, an unfair advantage. Birds often arrived back to the loft in groups. So whereas Les would normally stop timing in his birds after the first ten or twelve, ETS would mean that he and his pigeons would be likely to take the first twenty or thirty places in a race, in turn discouraging other fanciers from competing.

'But to be honest,' said Les, 'it won't make that much difference 'cause ours come back in batches anyway and we are always in the top place there or thereabouts. And anyway it's about setting standards to be the best.'

As Ray finished the boxing and checking he certainly couldn't see the benefit of continuing with the old ring system.

'They think 'cause they are called Royal they are royal,' Ray said, warming his hands around a mug of coffee. 'The RPRA think they have something to do with royalty and they have that snobbish attitude. It's ridiculous. They'll all be there at Blackpool. All for nowt, as they always are. All on expenses. All the hotel paid, the fuel bill paid the lot and the way they act is like a bunch of fuckin' pricks. They are not in the real world of pigeons. They never have been.'

'Would you like a midget gem?' said Les. He was happy now the pigeons were boxed up and merrily cooing in the back of the van. 'You can't beat the midget gems,' he said, stuffing a couple of green ones into his mouth before hitting the road to Blackpool. 'Bag of yer favourites. You can't beat that.'

Les seemed a little more sanguine now the laborious tasks were over but I sensed he was not entirely at peace. Bird flu was still lurking in the bushes of all things pigeon-related, like a serial flasher with an itchy trigger finger, ready to expose itself and cause minor shock and horror at any moment. Les had been disturbed by a letter he'd received from the Blackpool borough council during the week leading up to the convention. It was almost enough to put him off his midget gems.

'They've sent a letter and they were on the phone about nine times yesterday saying I've got to do this and that about the hygiene,' he said with a look of sheer disgust at the inconvenience of it all. 'That's what all that stuff is in the back there.' He was pointing to the cans of disinfectant rattling around next to the pigeon boxes. 'I've got to spray the cages with all that shit, but not only that

— I've got to have a written contingency plan too.'

According to the letter he'd received from the Blackpool council Les had to give bio-security advice to all those who purchased a pigeon in case of a bird flu outbreak. Which meant that the names, addresses and contact numbers of everyone at the auction had to be logged.

'Can you believe that? That's what they told me yesterday, a day before the fuckin' sale.' Les stuffed another handful of the midget gems in his mouth.

''I don't think you know what you are asking me to do.' I told 'em. 'I'm in the Savoy hotel. It's fuckin' massive. I'm on the microphone, on the stage. I don't know who's gonna come in and out of there. It's a public fuckin' place!' They said, 'You're the named organizer. It is part of your conditions of licence that you do that. If you don't do it we will have to shut you down.'

'This is the borough council of Blackpool,' said Les, his eyes wide in mock horror as we drove. 'The Blackpool fuckin' borough council! So I says to 'em, 'Listen, Stuart,' Stuart his name was, 'Stuart, I'm not saying I won't do it, but I can't do it. You are asking me to get the names and addresses of people who have nothing to do with pigeons. There

166

will be people in the hotel who could be walking through, who could just be there to meet somebody. They might 'ave just popped their heads in to have a look what's going on, or they might be on a dirty weekend away from the missus. If I start going around asking for names and addresses they might just tell me to fuck off. I cannot comply to that rule. It's a stupid fuckin' rule, mate.'

' 'I'll get back to DEFRA,' he says, 'I'll have to get their advice on that one. But you need to give everybody bio-security advice.' I said, 'Listen, mate, I'm from Salford, so I haven't got a fuckin' clue what that means.' He started laughing on the phone. I said, 'No, I'm being serious what the fuck's bio-security whatever?'

' 'Well, erm, you know you should advise people what to do when they are buying a pigeon and you must have a plan of attack in case of an outbreak. If the pigeon dies.'

'I said, 'I know you should never say never, but I've done hundreds of auctions and I've never had a pigeon die yet, and if a pigeon was going to die I'd know about it now. It wouldn't be coming with me.'

' 'Well you've got to do it,' he says. 'You've got to have a written contingency plan.'

'I thought, 'This is just bollocks!' so I sat down yesterday to write this plan and I thought what am I going to write? I haven't got a clue what to write. So I ring him back and tell him I haven't got a clue what to write and what do I do when I've wrote it?

' 'Nothing. You've just got to have it on you just in case we've got to see it,' says this Stuart bloke.

'So I sat up till twenty past eleven last night fuckin' typin' one of them contingency plans out. Fuckin' load of shite. I went on that DEFRA website to see how they worded it. I just copied it off them. So all their agents are going to be down there this weekend making sure I'm complying. 'Cause they'll use it as an excuse to stop us racing. If we don't comply this weekend they'll say, 'Oh they never complied at the show when they start racing. They're not going to comply again.' So that's what they're lookin' for. It's about being responsible on my behalf. I can only do my bit. There's fifty bastard auctions there and they can't all comply. Another thing is I've gotta have a vet on call. So I said, 'A vet on call for the weekend?' He says, 'Yeah, a vet on call who you can phone up for advice or who will attend your sale at any given moment in the event of an outbreak.' I said, 'My sales will go on till ten o'clock at night. How much do you think it would cost to have a vet on call until that time? It'll cost me about £700, so who's gonna pay that?' 'Well that's the condition of your licence,' he says.

' 'Well, are you gonna pay it? 'Cause I can't pay it. I can't pay £700 for a vet just to be there in the unlikely event that I need 'em.' So I phone up a vet that I use. They fucked me right off on the phone.

' 'Right,' says the vet, 'let me stop you right there, you're getting silly now, you pigeon people. I can't comply with that. I can't commit for a whole weekend. I just can't do it.'

'I thought 'fuckin' great stuff'. So I got this other vet who's being used at the show, and she says 'I can't be in two places at once.'

'I told her, 'The chances of me calling you are a million to one. Even if we have an outbreak I will not phone yer. I've just got to say I've phoned you 'cause if I can't say that I've phoned yer, they're gonna close me down.'

'She said, 'You definitely won't phone me?'

' 'Will I fuck phone yer. I won't phone yer if ten pigeons die.'

'So she took my name and I took hers and I banged her name down on my contingency plan. I mean, what is a vet going to do if something did happen? They would come out and say, 'Yes, Mr Green, that pigeon is dead.' 'Well, thanks very fuckin' much for that. There's your £700.''

That childhood sickly giddy feeling wasn't there as I saw Blackpool Tower appearing through the mist. Just the sickly bit. Probably too many midget gems.

'There she is!' said Les like Melville's Ishmael on sighting the great white whale Moby Dick. 'The Big Savoy!'

The Savoy was our home for the weekend, for Les, me and hundreds of other pigeon men. Les had been there so many times before that he now received a discount.

From the outside the Savoy looked good. It had a certain early twentieth-century austere grandness — I was told by a local it had been built in 1915 — that conjured up thoughts of dance bands and debutantes and a nostalgic whiff of St Bruno pipe tobacco, cream teas and Brylcreem. Very civilized. I asked Les if anybody famous had stayed there.

'I don't fuckin' know to be honest,' said Les. 'Although I think somebody saw Jimmy Cricket here a few years back.' He parked the van and we stepped outside. It was cold and the wind was hurricane standard. 'Bit parky innit?' he shivered.

A large man in a sheepskin and with very red cheeks was inside the hotel entrance smoking a cigarette. As we approached I nodded and smiled but he didn't nod or smile back. He just flicked his fag end in the direction of a brindle bull terrier that was squatting, with eyes squinting against the wind, and unloading its bowels just outside the door.

'Should be a good crack this,' said Les as we walked past the squatting dog and its red-cheeked owner.

Les was mobbed by a herd of pigeon fanciers as soon we stepped into the Savoy. A motley bunch garbed in leather jackets, woolly jumpers and wellies raced from the bar to greet the great pigeon man.

'Fuckin' 'ell, Les. They've not even got our rooms booked yet,' groaned one of the men.

Les had booked the rooms for around thirty of his pigeon pals. But he looked unruffled by the early complaints. This was Blackpool, everything was good. He took it all in his stride before joining me at the check-in desk.

'£120, please,' said a pale and unsmiling woman with a gap between her front teeth and an unnerving fury behind her small pale-blue eyes.

'£120?' I turned to Les with a look of incredulity.

Les smiled and shrugged.

'£120,' repeated the woman.

171

It wasn't a good start. 'Is that right?' I asked Les. He just smiled and shrugged again.

'How long are you staying?' she asked.

Two nights.

'Sorry, no, that'll be a £124 then.'

I reluctantly handed over the money and the woman took it without a smile and passed me the key to the room. 'Two flights up,' she said. 'But you'll have to use the stairs 'cause the lifts are being repaired.'

Bittersweet Blackpool. It was good to be back.

11

It isn't what it used to be

Live in the sunshine, swim the sea, drink the wild air.

Ralph Waldo Emerson

The hurricane wind was still rattling the windows of the Savoy and the bar was twenty-deep with pigeon men and half a dozen pigeon wives and girlfriends. There was now no escape. And Les had been right about one thing: I'd never seen as many bad outfits in my life.

The crowd in the Savoy bar looked like the dregs from an over-forties rave. Tracksuits seemed to be the fashionable choice for the youngish to middle-aged pigeon man. Tracksuits, football shirts and vests. These were usually worn with a shaven head, white trainers, tattoos and a black leather bomber jacket to keep out those biting Blackpool winds — gold sovereign rings were optional. The older pigeon gent, when not ensnaring himself in the tracksuit and leather, was a little more traditional in his tastes, mostly opting for the polyester slacks — in grey, stone and wine — pastel-coloured V-neck sweater and anorak combo, with flat cap and silver-rimmed cab driver's bifocals optional. Unfortunately the green leather jacket and the piano tie seemed to be out of season. But who was looking? This was no fashion show.

Whatever the garb, most were guzzling lager and sucking and wheezing on cigars, cigarettes and pipes, and every last shaven-headed and bespectacled one of them was talking pigeons.

'Pigeons, pigeons, pigeons' was all you could hear. All around me and everywhere I looked someone was mouthing the word 'pigeons'. Accents from every nook and cranny of merry old Britain, plus a few from Germany and Holland thrown in for a laugh, could be heard talking shop. It was a pigeon convention, I reasoned, so what did I expect? Not much, but this was *too* much. And when the screeching of the pigeon hordes became something like the screams of the damned, I began to think that I'd made a big mistake. What was I doing there? Without thinking it through. I'd somehow been swept along with the ridiculous notion that pigeon racing could benefit my life in some way. Did I really need this? 'Pigeons, pigeons, pigeons'. There lies the banter of the madhouse, the cuckoo's nest. Or the pigeon's nest. But those big, red-faced pigeon men were loving it. They thought it was fine. ETS, one-loft races, who were the best — the cocks or the hens? The debates raged on. They thought it was OK, in fact better than OK. They were loving every minute of it. 'Pigeons, pigeons, pigeons' they all said a thousand times or more.

'You'll love it here tonight,' said John as he stood drinking and smoking at the bar. 'It's full of half-wits.'

John was another one of Les's pigeon pals. He was one of the young up and comers in the game at only thirty, but he'd won pigeon races, lots of them. John was a star in the making and he was also a well-schooled expert in the art of taking the piss, as most Salfordians often are.

'Some right cranks here tonight,' said John, staring at a small, pale man with a goatee beard who was struggling with a crate of brown ale behind the bar. 'You must hate your job, you!' John shouted at the man.

The man dropped the crate, turned and smiled nervously, but said nothing. 'You were here last year and you didn't look happy then,' added John, winking at me and taking a good drag of his Embassy no. 5. 'You should find yourself another job, mate. Cheer yourself up a bit.'

I hadn't had a drink for several weeks but I suddenly decided that I needed one.

'You look nervous,' said John. 'Are you all right?'

'Yes,' I replied, 'I'm great.'

Les was up on stage in the ballroom, under the glitter ball that hung from the peach and turquoise ceiling, doing what he did best: selling pigeons to pigeon men. Like I said before, very few people in this world sold pigeons better than Les. He was a master up on that stage. He had presence and the crowd appreciated it. They rarely moved their bloodshot gazes from the stocky, swaggering figure in the blue button-down shirt, and they laughed in all the right places.

'This pigeon is a real investment,' said Les of Lot no. 1, a grey hen. 'Like buying a house.' He was off again, but this time his voice was in fine fettle and the stage was bigger than the Steelworkers' Club in Irlam. This was, after all, the 'Night of The Stars'.

The place was packed and it was standing room only. But apart from Les, the stars — Koopman and the other Dutch and Belgian champions — were absent. What with bird flu and the weather, they had probably chosen warmer climes for a weekend break. But nobody seemed to care whether they were there or not. Everybody realized the real

176

stars were the seventy-two pigeons sat in those cages in front of the stage. Anyway most of the crowd were drunk, especially the man who suddenly crowbarred himself into a space next to me at the back of the room. 'Eric,' he introduced himself. Eric said he was from the Isle of Man, and with lager in hand and grin on his chubby face he looked as if all his birthdays had come at once.

'You should cheer up, mate,' he shouted to me over the racket. 'It's a great weekend, this is. Smile. If you can't enjoy yourself here there's something wrong with yer.' I was always suspicious of the uninvited stranger who was keen to point out the joys of living. They were often the closet depressives, those just one false step on the tightrope away from a nasty fall. But I gave Eric the benefit of the doubt. He was maybe just trying to be friendly and he was a bit pissed. 'This is Blackpool, mate,' he said before bouncing off for another beer. 'Enjoy yourself.' This was Blackpool. Where all your troubles were left outside with the gale force winds and the squatting brindle bull terrier.

'Everybody loves a red cock,' said Les suggestively, before pointing to a red cock in a cage on a table in front of the stage. The crowd laughed. 'Give your wife a belated Christmas present. This red cock is a beauty.

No better pigeon in here tonight.'

Bejewelled hands shot up and bids came faster than a Blackpool tram, and the red cock went for £200.

'You can't go wrong with this one,' said Les pointing to a grey hen. 'If this bird isn't going to set the world of pigeons alight, I don't know what is.' Les had seventy-two yearlings to sell. The prices ranged between £150 and £1,500, but sell them he did. From the red cock to the checker hen, as the winds blew the expletives flew, and the pigeon men supped and smoked. And Les sold the whole bloomin' lot in under three hours.

'Thank fuck for that,' he said as he walked off the stage and Pat boxed up the final pigeon and handed it to its new rotund owner.

'Did you do well, Les?' I asked him.

'Not bad at all, as it goes. Now where's the fuckin' bar?'

The Night of the Stars was over but the serious work had only just begun for Les and the other pigeon men. The work they'd been looking forward to. And that work was drinking alcohol. It was work Les and his pals enjoyed and they did it very well.

I'd had sessions with big drinkers before. I'd spent a whole night and an early morning drinking with members of the New Jersey mob. They were all big men and big drinkers but I'd held my own. I'd drunk with Scottish navvies, Bulgarian drug dealers and Irish travellers, and managed to find my way home without me or anyone else having to call for help. But the pigeon man was a different beast altogether. When it came to guzzling booze the pigeon man was in a league of his own.

Booze and the pigeon man were old friends. They went back a long way. Like the darts player, the pigeon man had a special relationship with ale. They looked out for each other.

I'd had a plan of sorts. That was why I'd made the trip. I thought, dazzled by the bright lights of Blackpool, I could get Les to commit to the South African race and also throw in a few potential young champion pigeons for good measure. It was a simple plan but not a great one as I'd overlooked one crucial detail. Les and his mates could drink like bastards.

Every drink that came my way in the early stages of the marathon session that late January night in Blackpool was at least a treble — the pigeon man was a generous sort — and after six or seven I thought I'd suffered a minor stroke. The right side of my face stopped working for several hours and I started to float rather than walk, in a raggedy, wibbly wobbly kind of way, like a Thunderbirds puppet. As Les and the pigeon men began to build up a steady rhythm to their drinking, a fast-paced bossa nova style rhythm, it was all I could do to remain upright and listen to a pal of Les's talk about the time they had worked at a fish market together.

'Do you remember the bloke who nicked that fish?' said Les's chum as my head swirled and the drinks flowed. I laughed and Les and all the pigeon men laughed too. We were all having a great time and the story about the stolen fish unfolded, but very soon so did I. The effect of the drinks suddenly swept over me like a magician's cape and I reappeared sometime later in my room without even a murmur to Les about the big race.

★　★　★

The Saturday morning of the National Pigeon Racing Convention 2006 was a harsh and terrible morning for me. Outside the sun was shining and the wind had dropped, but even though my wind had also dropped I wasn't shining. In fact I was very overcast indeed. The many whiskies I'd consumed the night before were disagreeing with me quite badly and I'd started to discover things that I hadn't discovered in all the excitement of the day before. A few little things that were making the morning a bit more uncomfortable. First of all, after a lengthy and sweaty search, I found out that I'd somehow lost a shoe. A desert boot to be precise, and one that I was fond of and I'd been wearing quite happily the night before. Also during the search it dawned on me that the room I'd forked out £62 a night for was like something you'd find down a dark backstreet in Bucharest.

In a nutshell it was grim. It was dark and dingy, with a view directly onto a brick wall, and there was an old creaky brown wardrobe and a grubby chair with graffiti on it — somebody had penned a cock and balls into the flowery pattern. The room was clammy, cloyingly warm, smelt of old talcum powder, the window didn't open and, thrown in for no extra charge, it was right next to a generator of some description that was groaning loudly.

I wasn't in the best shape and if I never heard the word 'pigeon' again I would have been very happy. But the room wasn't inviting me to stay; in fact it was telling me to piss off out of it. I didn't feel good but I tried to rescue the situation so I phoned down to reception to complain and request a new room.

'We can't move you. The hotel is full, sir, because of the pigeon convention.' It was the woman with the fury behind her eyes. She didn't sound overly concerned about my plight. 'I can bring you a fan, though, if that helps with the heat.' I told her not to worry herself, that it didn't matter, I wasn't planning on hanging around in the room anyway.

Les was arguing with a man in a black waistcoat and tie who was dishing out the breakfast in the dining room when I arrived. Les wanted extra bacon and the man said he'd had his full quota. 'All the money I spend in this place and I can't even get an extra bit of fuckin' bacon!' Les fumed as he sat down next to Pat. Pat had demolished his breakfast and looked disappointed that he'd now be hard pressed to go up for seconds.

'You look terrible,' Pat said to me as he stood and hitched up his very baggy trackuit bottoms over his gut. 'I've been on the drink for days and look at me.'

After toying with a cold egg I decided not to hang around with Les and the lads. I wasn't feeling well enough and it looked as if the bar wasn't too far from their minds. I got out of there and checked to see if anyone had handed in my desert boot. 'No,' said the woman helpfully. There was only one thing for it. When at a loss, head for the Winter Gardens and the *British Homing World* Show of the Year.

A late winter sun poked through the clouds and illuminated the pavements and the white hotel façades as I walked along the sea front. For a moment I felt slightly better and Blackpool looked almost as bright and shiny as I'd remembered it as a kid. Like a thin smear of make-up on an ageing dolly bird, the sun gave Blackpool a momentary hint of its former low-rent glamour. But it didn't last. As I walked down the North Pier towards the South it became depressingly obvious that all was not well with Blackpool. The grand-looking hotels on the front that once gleamed and looked classy and expensive were now peeling and cracked, and practically pleaded with you to come in. There was something quite nightmarish about it. Like the ghostly figure of Miss Haversham in *Great Expectations* sitting under the cobwebs with her memories and her bitterness, Blackpool seemed to be slowly and regretfully fading away.

As I continued walking a sallow-faced man stepped out of the Cherry Blossom guest house carrying a black bin liner stuffed with what appeared to be his worldly possessions, shaking his head and talking to himself. I don't think he was one of the pigeon fanciers although I could have been wrong. He was quickly followed by a middle-aged woman with hair like straw, who looked like she'd been crying. The woman caught up with the man and they argued and fought on the prom until the woman sat down in the middle of the road and sobbed.

It went on. Many of the small guest houses off the front where I'd stayed as a kid were now home to the lost and the desperate during the off-season months. They now stood forlornly next to shabby novelty shops selling crotchless panties alongside Blackpool rock, and the many secondhand shops, with fridges and cookers piled up on the pavements outside to cater for the flotsam of this depressing new kind of bedsit land. Blackpool had been in decline for many years — since the advent of the cheap package deal and the desire for somewhere more exotic — but the rot looked as if it had set in for good.

Despite the declining numbers taking part in pigeon racing, the *British Homing World* Show of the Year at the Winter Gardens was still one of the busiest weekends in Blackpool. The show covered the entire complex from

184

the grand old Opera House to the Empress Ballroom, and each venue was full of stalls selling anything from £25,000 mahogany lofts to pigeon teapots.

I shoehorned myself into a cafe where the pigeon man was once again in attendance. 'It isn't what it used to be,' said the man stood next to me as I ordered my coffee. He didn't look very well. He was a big man but he was pale and had a terrible cough. He was wearing a T-shirt under his sheepskin coat that said: 'Blackpool Pigeon Show. I'm Only Here For The Birds and Booze'.

'How do you mean?' I asked.

'It's not like it was. Big money in pigeons now. The innocence has gone from the game.'

I bought him a tea and he told me his name was Eamonn. Eamonn was a traveller and had been involved with pigeons in one way or another for over forty-five years, until he was forced to stop due to his unfortunate condition. He told me he had what is known in the pigeon racing trade as PFL, or pigeon fanciers lung — a respiratory problem correctly called Extrinsic Allergic Alveolitis that was believed to be linked to working in enclosed pigeon lofts over long periods.

'I've had it for nearly two years now,' said Eamonn. 'That's what they think it is anyway. Pigeon lung. I've had blood tests and they

185

think it's because of the pigeons. Put it this way, I cough me bastard guts up if I go anywhere near the things.'

'Shouldn't you be as far away from here as possible, then?'

'I can't help it. I can't stay away from the pigeons. It's hard to stay away when you've been involved with them as long as I have,' said Eamonn.

Representatives from the Pigeon Fanciers Medical Research Centre were somewhere in the Winter Gardens and Eamonn wanted to see them and get their advice. He wanted to know if there was anything that could be done to improve his condition or anything in existence that could help him get back in the loft. I had no plan of action so I told Eamonn I'd help him find them.

'You can see how much people are making out of it, can't yer?' he pointed out as we walked past stalls and show stands selling all manner of pigeon paraphernalia: medical supplies, pigeon portraits, pigeon T-shirts and DVDs. 'Like I say. Big business now.'

Eamonn had a point. None of the stuff was cheap. Not that I was an expert, but £25 for a pigeon cruet set seemed a bit steep. Eamonn's cough got worse when we walked through the Empress Ballroom. It was probably something to do with the fact that there were around 2,000 show pigeons in there that had all competed in the 'Crufts of the Pigeon world' the day before.

'It kills me to walk past these little buggers,' said Eamonn, quickening his step past the cages that housed the show birds — mostly white pigeons, beautifully coloured with flecks of anything from beige to burgundy. 'Lovely things, aren't they?' he said as we rushed through.

We walked around the Winter Gardens several times but couldn't find the pigeon lung experts. After the third circuit Eamonn didn't seem to be too concerned. He decided that a drink was probably the best way to soothe his condition. We pitched up at the bar and he seemed to improve with a pint of Guinness in his hand. 'I'm hopeful of a cure,' he told me, slurping on the black stuff. 'Amazing things can be done in this day and age: heart transplants, separate Siamese twins, Dolly the Sheep an' all that stuff . . . ' But soon, after a couple more pints, Eamonn's optimism was replaced with a dark cloud of melancholia.

'You don't know what you've got until it isn't there any more.' He was wistfully staring at a stand selling, bizarrely, portraits of Elvis and John Wayne. 'The best years of my life were spent with the pigeons, and now look at me. I've been cursed with this bastard thing,' he said pointing to his chest.

I wasn't sure how serious pigeon lung was as Eamonn was the first person I'd ever met with the condition. I didn't know what to say. 'It's not life threatening, is it?' I asked.

'Nahh. I'll be around for a while yet, don't you worry about that. But to never handle a pigeon again? That's a hard thing to happen to yer. To never spend time in the loft with your grandchildren? Let's hope they find a cure for it out there, eh?' He finished his pint and wandered off towards the Empress Ballroom.

Les and the boys were in the bar of the big Savoy when I finally found them. I could see the back of John's head and hear him hassling another barman, this time a small myopic Irishman with thick-rimmed spectacles who'd got the order wrong.

'He wanted a Stella, his was a Bud, mine was a Stella, his was a half . . . you want to get those specs looked at, my old cocker. They don't seem to be helping.' I could hear the insults over the early evening pigeon chatter. Les was sat not far away from the bar holding court with several men who were laughing very loudly at whatever he was saying. For a moment I was tempted to find out but I thought better of it. This was

188

Blackpool, a place for fun and frolics and four-in-the-morning pigeon chatter but I'd had my fill. My grim room suddenly seemed as inviting as a suite at the Dorchester. I left the pigeon men to it, climbed the stairs and put the key in the off-white door. The smell of musty talc filled my nostrils but I didn't care. Inside on the table there was a message from the woman with the fury behind her eyes. 'See reception. Found shoe.' Suddenly I was in love with Blackpool again.

12

Some of us are looking at the drains

'I couldn't believe it was going to crash. I thought it would go on forever. But I was just a pigeon.'

Walter Annenberg

There was no room for sentiment when it came to pigeon flying. You had to be ruthless if you wanted to be successful. 'If a pigeon can't fly then it's in the pie,' Frank said, or in Les's words, 'If it can't get its arse in, it's in the fuckin' bin'.

The racing pigeon was an incredible creature, however, as Andrew Blechman described with great clarity and style in his book *Pigeons*:

With hollow bones containing reservoirs of oxygen, a tapered fuselage, giant breast muscles that account for one third of its body mass, and an ability to function indefinitely without sleep, the rock dove is a feathered rocket built for speed and endurance. If an average up-and-down of the wing takes a bird three feet, then a racer is making roughly 900,000 of those motions during a long-distance race, while maintaining 600 heartbeats per minute — triple its resting heart rate. The rock dove can reach peak velocity in seconds and maintain it for hours on end. One pigeon was recorded flying for several hours at 110mph — an Olympian feat by any measure.

On average the pigeon races for four years and can live for over twenty, but the average life expectancy for the pigeon in captivity, i.e. the racing pigeon, is fourteen years. The feral bird, with its diet of chips and burgers and street scraps, is not expected to live beyond four years old. Generally speaking, however, the majority of Les's birds were 'in the bin' (dead) before they'd reached five years old. It was only the lucky cocks (the hens were usually no good for breeding after the age of ten at best) who reached anything like the grand age of fourteen.

'No point in keeping 'em if they aren't any good,' Les always said. 'You can't sell pigeons to people if they aren't decent. They'll never buy anything off yer again. And with the breeding it's like anything in life: the older you get, the more useless you become.'

Moonie was thinking of nothing else and he had a dilemma. He only had a dozen pigeons left, after losing the majority of them over the business with the neighbours and his loft, and as the pigeons grew and started to fly he found out that none of them were up to scratch. They were pretty good birds, from good stock, but Moonie just didn't have the energy or the money to keep them fed and looked after the way they needed to be. He had to make the choice: keep them for fun or get rid of them.

'I think that's the end of me and pigeons now,' he said regretfully over the phone one night just before the new season. 'I don't think it's any good me trying to kid m'self. I'm just not up to bein' in the loft every day.'

Moonie needed something to keep him occupied other than the nook of the Star public house. He was seventy-four years old and the pigeons, whether they could fly or not, were a good way to get him out of the house, so I told him to keep his birds. What did it matter if he didn't race them? Moonie couldn't compete with the Leses of this world anyhow. Nobody expected his birds to be world beaters, but why not fly them for the sake of it?

'You think so?' I could tell by the tone of his voice that that was the answer he wanted to hear, but he still protested half-heartedly. 'I thought I told you I'd give you some birds for the race. I don't want to let you down, kid.'

I'd known for months I wouldn't be sending any of Moonie's pigeons to South Africa. I'd just been in denial and I was hoping that the race might be moved to a later date because of bird flu, giving me more time to scrounge the money together and persuade Les to enter. No such luck. Despite the discovery of a mute swan in Fife which was thought to have the H5N1 strain, pigeons could still be sent to South Africa. The date for shipment was June 2006 and, as it was already March, the new racing season was nearly upon us. Time was running out, Les was still indifferent and I was broke.

For a while I'd been struggling to pay the rent due to lack of work and funds. I had no savings and what little work was dribbling in just about covered my food and bills. Chasing the pigeon dream was beginning to get in the way of the day-to-day management of my life, so not long after the chat with Moonie the moment that I'd been dreading and expecting arrived: a moment with all the charm of the bailiff at the door. Basically I had to find a job. If I was to carry on with the writing and have any chance of buying a pigeon and competing in the Million Dollar race, I had to get the debts and the landlord off my case.

There wasn't a great deal on offer in Manchester for the writer in his early thirties who specialized in boxing and had a vague knowledge of pigeon racing, but I needed something quick. I looked in local papers, even shuffled into the Job Centre once or twice, until the woman at the temp agency smiled a patronizing smile, gawped at her computer and offered me a job at a call centre. I wasn't that desperate so I did what I had done once before when things had been shit — I walked into the local bookies and asked if they were hiring.

The thing was, the bookies were always hiring. The smoke-, aggression- and depression-filled environment of the turf accountant was an unhealthy place to work, so they weren't exactly turning people away, and with the nation being encouraged to 'bet its bollocks', bookmakers' shops were mushrooming on every street corner. The bookies weren't fussy. They were always happy to see you whether you wanted to work for them or not. As long as you could count a bit and didn't want to steal their money, you were in. And so within three or four days I was earning five and a half quid an hour working as a cashier with a man called Keith who wore a bad wig — I suppose there aren't many good wigs — and a bookies' manager called Tom.

I had a job. Things were improving but it wasn't all cherries and roses. There were a few problems. I'd worked in a bookies before, some time in the mid nineties, and it had been a doddle. Back then as a lowly cashier you would take the betting slip from the customer, copy it on a scanner at your side, return one half of the slip to the customer and keep the other half to settle later if need be. It was easy. All the bets were settled by the manager. The cashier had only to take and dish out the money so after taking the bets you had time on your hands — time to watch the races, read a book or observe the punter either going nuts with joy having won, or consumed with fear and anger having lost.

The bookies had been a reasonable place to make a bit of money to keep the wolves at bay, but my first problem was this: things in the world of the cashier had changed since 1994. The photocopying scanner method had been given its marching orders and had been replaced by a computerized system. I wasn't against progress but the system wasn't better for the lowly cashier. Each bet had to be typed into the computer, the computer logged it and if the bet was a winning one the machine settled it. It made the manager's life easier but it made the low-paid cashier's life harder.

The bookies I found myself in was one of the busiest in North Manchester so basically it was non-stop. When I wasn't taking bets — around 300 a day — I was sat hunch-backed on a high stool typing bets into the computer. Apart from the racing on the telly, it wasn't much better than the call centre. I had little time to think, and I was trapped behind the bullet-proof glass until I could nick half an hour for my lunch.

The other problem was Tom. 'Pigeon racing. Poor man's fookin' horse racing. Sport for wankers, that,' he said after I foolishly told him why I was trying to scrape some money together.

'Don't mind Tom,' said Keith, his silver-grey wig glinting under the bright lights. 'That's just his way.'

And Tom's way was the wrong way. Leaving aside many of his other foibles (and there were many), Tom was a racist. He wasn't just 'a bit thick' and he didn't lack the education to articulate his frustrations, he was a full-on racist. He didn't like foreigners and especially those of a different colour. 'Watch out for the coloureds who come in 'ere,' he had said on my first morning on the job. 'They can't be trusted.'

There were many people, I found out as the days and then weeks dragged by, who couldn't be trusted in that smoke-filled betting shop, but as far as I could see through the smoke the half a dozen or so black or Asian men who occasionally had a bet were the least corrupt of the denizens.

I suppose I should have walked out as soon as Tom had opened his dumb mouth. I could have got a job at any number of bookies if I'd made the effort, but I didn't. This wasn't a long-term career move, I needed the money and the bookies was just around the corner from where I lived so I could get up a little later in the morning. Working with a racist — where was my pride? I didn't feel good about it, but it would be my cross to bear for a while.

I wasn't the only one who was having difficulties, though. Moonie's problems just kept piling up. No sooner had he given his pigeons a stay of execution than his beloved dog Gregg died. Gregg was fifteen years old, not a bad age for a dog and a few years on a pigeon, but Moonie loved him and Gregg's death hit him hard. Not long after I found out, and thinking he needed cheering up with tales of the bookies, I paid him a visit. I told him about Keith's wig and Tom's bigotry and one of our more chatty regular punters who'd spent fifteen years inside for murdering his wife, but it didn't seem to work and I began to worry. Pigeons aside, I was afraid that Moonie was on the verge of giving in altogether.

All of the pigeon men I'd met had good qualities, despite their quirks and roguish natures. From Les and Ray to Frank and Paul, and all the others in between, I got the impression that these men had a sense of decency, self respect and pride in what they did. Those qualities that sounded old-fashioned and corny but were as rare as Bengal tigers in Bury. There was a strong character lurking under all those loft coats, scruffy jumpers, bravado and pigeon chat. Moonie was the same. He was a tough old bird, and he'd had a pretty hard life. He'd dealt with the death of his wife and the disappointment of unfulfilled ambitions with grace and a sense of optimism and humour.

But that afternoon I realized that Moonie's spirit was breaking. He looked tired and defeated, like an old man with nowhere to go. He sat in front of the TV watching *Deal or No Deal* and the like, hardly moving for three or four hours. It was clear from the state of the house that he hadn't done much in the way of cooking and cleaning for a couple of weeks. Even Lou the foul-mouthed parrot was keeping his mouth shut. I guess even he could sense that something was not quite right.

'Have you ever heard of GI Joe?' said Moonie after a nearly an hour of silence. I told him I hadn't. 'GI Joe was a pigeon who saved the lives of over a thousand British troops during the Second World War. These British troops had captured an Italian city from the Germans but nobody knew they had done it and the Americans were going to bomb it 'cause they thought it was full of Germans. So, thinking that after all that they were going to be bombed by their own allies, one of the British soldiers noticed this pigeon that they'd brought with them. It was a carrier pigeon so they stuck a message to it saying not to bomb the town and they let him go. All those lives depended on that pigeon and he flew through bombs and fire and the lot and got to the other side just before the Americans were going to set off. Saved the lot of 'em. A wonderful thing, the pigeon,' said Moonie.

'He won the animal version of the Victoria Cross (Dickin Medal) for that, did GI Joe, and he's stuffed in a museum now. Amazing what animals can do for people. He sat there with a sad look on his face. We are all in the gutter, but some of us are looking at the drains,' he continued mournfully, before locking his gaze back on to *Who Wants to Be a Millionaire?*

I didn't know what it all meant. GI Jo and Oscar Wilde? But it didn't sound good. That night I rang Frank and told him I was worried about his old mate. 'I'll make some calls,' Frank said. 'One thing about the pigeon men is they always stick together. They look out for each other. If one of their own is struggling, they'll help him out with pigeons or money or whatever he wants. They're a good lot that way.'

One man who wasn't one of the 'good lot' was Tom. Tom was becoming the bane of my life and I'd begun to despise him. The pigeon racing world had its share of lunkheads and bigots like anywhere else, but on the whole they were the kind of working-class people who cared about something, even if it was only pigeons. They had a passion and educated themselves to be as good as they could be. Tom didn't seem to care or know very much about anything. Even horse racing, which he'd been surrounded by five days a week for over thirty years of his life, was still a big mystery to him.

Tom would occasionally give a tip to some of the less clued-up punters. Never the staff, which was just as well. 'You wanna get on Black Cloud in the two-forty. Rat up a fookin' drain pipe, that horse is.' A rat would have fared better than one of Tom's tips. I'm sure he must have had some winners but I never saw any. He was the worst tipster I'd seen.

It was inevitable things would come to a head between him and me. There was a nag called Liberty Seeker which was running in the two-fifty from Catterick on a wet Wednesday in early April. There were several regular biggish-money gamblers in the shop and despite none of them being foreigners, all of them were untrustworthy, and all were on the lookout for a free ride.

It was an old trick and I should have been more alert. Confuse the cashier, wait for the rush and give him several bets and a bit of money and tell him to pay the bets off the winnings that are owed. This punter had so many bets on the go — despite the foolproof computer login system — that I panicked and somehow gave him a free bet for sixty pounds. I knew what I'd done within minutes and I asked the man for the money back, but he refused.

'I paid you the money,' he said. I shut down the till and cashed up. It was sixty pounds light but he still refused to give me the money. Against my better judgement, I sought Tom out for advice. It was a problem easily solved with a calm head and reasoning so I thought that he was just the man.

'What 'ave I told you about watchin' what yer doin', eh?' Tom wasn't happy and started to go red and shout. I'd just given him an opportunity to show off his power. The shop turned over thousands in profit every day so they weren't short of sixty pounds. It was a bookmakers, for Christ's sake. 'What did ah fookin' tell yer, eh? Keep yer eye on all this lot.'

'I thought you said keep your eye on the coloureds,' I said.

'Don't worry about it,' Keith reassured me. 'It will all blow over.'

'Like your wig in a strong wind,' I thought. Keith meant well. But I would have paid more attention if he hadn't been wearing that terrible vanity rug. In the end I left without much fuss. I wanted to punch some sense into Tom but I would have been there for a long time before any of it materialized. I needed the cash, but I left that day and didn't return. I couldn't deal with Tom any longer and I had no desire to wake up one morning and find myself goose-stepping to the bookies. I'd made enough money to keep me going for a month and that would have to do.

★　★　★

The terrible news came a week later. It was another grey and wet day in Manchester and, despite the apparent onset of global warming, the winter weather was lingering as it often did up north. I was in the vegetable department of Tesco's looking for a cabbage when Frank called my mobile.

'He's passed away, son. Moonie's gone.'

I hadn't known Moonie for long but had really liked the daft old sod, and I felt sad when Frank told me the news. He had died of a heart attack during a short spell in hospital. It wasn't the best way to go but I guess it wasn't the worst either.

I attended the funeral a few days later, which was a quiet one by Irish Catholic standards. Moonie, Frank told me, had fallen out with a lot of his family so there was a small turnout. Moonie's sister and two of his sons attended, plus a few of his pals from the Star including the landlord, Steve the Oracle, and Frank who bought a wreath in the shape of a pigeon.

We all went back to the Star afterwards where Frank said he was going to look after Lou the parrot, while Steve said he was going to look after what was left of the pigeons in Moonie's loft. Then we all got drunk and listened to Moonie's favourite,

Elvis Presley, and some of us sang and some of us cried. Frank didn't do either, though — after all, there's no room for sentiment in pigeon racing.

13

You can't win 'em all

Accept that some days you're the pigeon and some days you're the statue.

Anonymous

Moonie had left Frank and me a solid silver pigeon each for luck, and as the 2006 season started, the gods of good fortune began to smile on me for the first time in a while. I had a new girlfriend and I was offered some well-paid work by a TV company, who wanted me to help them make a show about a boxer, and Les sounded as if he'd had a change of heart about the South African race. How could my life possibly improve from there?

'Should be able to sort you with some pigeons, no problem, mate,' said Les in a surprising expletive-free moment.

I wondered what was wrong with Les. It was as if our earlier conversations about the one-loft race had never happened, but I wasn't complaining. I guessed the sanguine mood was something to do with the success he'd tasted in the early part of the season. Les and the team had got off to a flyer, as they always did, dominating the leading positions in the Oldham Federation. They were also happy, or as happy as they could be, with the restrictions DEFRA had placed on the early part of the pigeon racing season due to the dreaded bird flu. DEFRA had deemed it necessary to stop pigeons flying out of the UK — no flights to or from France — but this didn't bother Les. He wasn't a big fan of overseas flying anyway.

'Fuckin' great for us, to be honest, 'cause our birds don't like flying across water anyway,' Les had said on the phone with a hint of a smile in his voice.

I arranged to meet him at the loft on a race day, my plan being to get him to finally commit to the Million Dollar race. It was a gamble — what if he lost and he changed his mind? — but it was worth a punt and, besides, I'd never seen Les and his pigeons do what they did best. Never seen the athletes of the sky in action. I'd only heard about the levels of tension and excitement that could be generated when man was waiting for racing pigeon to arrive back in loft.

'The excitement on a Saturday is unbeliev- able,' Les had told me, eyes on stalks and hardly pausing for breath as he gave me the inside track on a big race day. 'You go to your club on a Friday night and you have a list of all the pigeon ring numbers you are sending to the race. You give that to the secretary, and she takes each of your pigeons out of the basket and reads its number. She finds it on your sheet and then puts that special elasticated number next to it, so they know that it has gone to the race with that number on its leg. Then the wagon takes them to the liberation point.'

Les had had to stop and steady himself at that moment. I could see those familiar exhilarating feelings that ran through him like electric charges were beginning to buzz. This was December and he hadn't had that race-day feeling for a few months.

'When it comes home we are waiting here and when it comes into view, fuck me. When you see them come over on the horizon, fuckin' sixteen ounces of prime feather, just come from 200 miles, or maybe 500 miles across France, and when you shout at it and it comes flying through those doors, I know it sounds corny, but there is no better feeling; it's one of the greatest feelings you can have. And when you time it in and you know it's a winner and you check the dial and you know it's correct and you know that you've won it

. . . well, it really is a feeling you can't explain to people, it's an adrenaline rush. It's like the greatest orgasm you've ever fuckin' 'ad.'

The Portland combine was a big race for Les and the team. It was a race for young birds — two-year-olds — and Les had fifty of them flying approximately 250 miles back to Oldham, against 1,500 pigeons from the north-west of England. He had had success in the race before, winning it three times in the past five years. 'All the others who have won it that often have won it over a twenty-year period,' said Les as Pat, wearing a salmon-pink vest and a crucifix around his neck, fried something in a pan and Gary smoked a roll-up just outside the cabin.

The pigeons had been liberated at around 11.35 a.m. (Les had expected them to go earlier) and were due back at around two p.m. It was now one p.m. and Les was clearly agitated as he sipped eagerly at his tea and looked from the sky to the clock on the cabin wall and back again. 'How long 'ave I been doin' this?' Les asked no one in particular. 'And I still shit m'self. Still nervous on race day. Can't help it, just can't help it.' He was pacing like a man awaiting the electric chair.

Gary rolled his eyes and smiled at me. He lit another cigarette and answered the phone, which had been ringing on and off for an hour. 'Like it does every race day,' he'd said. The callers were pigeon men, some of them rivals and some of them friends, wanting to know if any birds had returned.

''Ave you 'ad any back yet?' Gary said to the voice on the other end of the phone. 'We 'aven't 'ad any back yet. 'Ave you 'ad any back yet?' Nobody had had any back yet.

Les left the cabin briefly, went to the loft and pulled out a pigeon. He then stood outside, stroking the pigeon, while staring out over the council houses at a blue sky liberally feathered with light clouds. It was a fine day but the wind was quite strong and in the distance I could see a hot air balloon zipping through the clouds. Les pointed towards it.

''Ave you fuckin' seen that? The wind is right up over there. Doesn't favour us today. Doesn't favour us at all. Favours the racers who are further away,' he said angrily and marched back to the cabin, still cradling the pigeon. The wind was a stiff west-north-westerly by all accounts, which meant the birds further away from where Les was situated in Oldham would be wind-assisted as they flew the last few miles home.

'This will sort 'em out,' said Les. 'It'll make pigeons out of 'em, this will. Sort out the men from the boys.'

I watched TV and then I wandered onto

the roof of the loft and stared at the car mechanics below messing about with an old Mercedes. This was the quietest, and the tensest, I'd seen Les. He was relatively mute, compared with the usual hyper, verbose Les, as he waited for the pigeons to return. There was hardly a sound on the roof apart from the clink clank of the mechanics' tools below and the faint noise of a police siren in the distance. 'Is it always like this?' I asked Gary. 'Oh aye, there's a lot of tension and hanging about, but it's great when they come. You'll see.'

I waited and grew bored. There was only so much looking at the sky, and at Les pacing around, that a man could do. There wasn't a great deal you could occupy yourself with as you waited; pigeon racing wasn't the greatest spectator sport. From what I'd experienced in the build-up it came some way below curling and draughts in the viewing stakes. I walked around a bit, watched Pat eat and smoke, and stared at the pigeons through the loft door. I walked about the roof some more, and found a grotesque colony of white dog shit behind the cabin. At least I'd found something to keep me occupied for a minute or two. I hadn't seen white dog shit since 1979.

'That's the dog that did that,' said Gary as I stared down at the crap.

I had gathered that. I didn't think it was Pat or Les. At least I hoped it wasn't. 'But why is it white?'

'The sun bleaches it,' said Gary, before walking off to look at the sky again.

'Ahh, thanks, Gary. I never knew that.' I felt quite pleased that an ancient mystery had been uncovered. At least the day wasn't a total waste.

'Stop acting the fuckin' goat over there,' Les shouted to me. He was somewhat fraught, being a bag of nerves on race day. 'I don't want you hanging about on the roof when they come back, you'll fuckin' scare 'em and they won't want to come in.' I knew he wasn't joking; I could see he was reaching breaking point. It was two-ish and they still weren't back, and his phone hadn't stopped ringing.

'You 'ad any back? We 'aven't 'ad any back yet.' Nobody had had any back yet. The gold medal was still up for grabs, despite Les's pessimism. They still had a chance. Les stared at the sky, shading his eyes from the sun, as did Gary and Pat. I left them to it and waited in the cabin in front of the telly. 'Here they come, Les! Here they come!' Pat shouted. I was suddenly jolted from my inertia.

Les squinted into the distance. 'That's a fuckin' seagull, you daft bastard.'

'Is it?'

More time elapsed. I made some tea for me and the gang. 'How do you take it?' I asked Pat. 'Up the arse,' he replied.

When a pigeon comes home from a race, you have to grab it as quickly as possible, take the elasticated band from its leg and place the band into a small plastic capsule. From there the capsule is placed into a tamperproof clock and the pigeon band is time-coded and stored for safekeeping. It is a pretty good system and very difficult to cheat, although Les, as he had argued before Blackpool and on many occasions, thought the ETS system was better for all concerned. Less stress for the pigeon as well as for the pigeon man with dodgy knees and shaky hands, etc.

I'd been on the roof of Les's loft since eleven a.m. It was now two-thirty p.m. I was making the tea so I didn't hear the cries of 'Here they fuckin' come!' from outside. It was only when Gary dashed into the cabin for the capsules he needed to time the pigeons into the loft that I realized it was all happening.

'They're here!' he said simply, before dashing out again. I dumped the tea and jogged after him. Outside Les was whistling and clucking the roof of his mouth with his tongue. Cluck, cluck, cluck. He had some feed in his hand and he was throwing it into the loft, trying to coax the pigeons that circled somewhere in the sky back into the loft.

'C'MON! C'MON!' Whistle, whistle, whistle; cluck, cluck, cluck. 'C'MON!' More feed was thrown into the loft. I looked skyward again, arching my back, craning my neck until it began to ache, but I couldn't see them. At one point I thought I saw something, but when I looked again it was gone, and it could have even been a seagull.

'Over there,' said Pat, pointing behind the loft. I turned and as I did, the pigeons moved, but again I didn't see them. Apparently they had swooped down into the loft. They were quick, very quick, like mercury with feathers, and they were swiftly followed by Gary and Les.

Gary was in and out of the loft in a flash. 'Two of 'em in,' he said, face red and grinning.

'Yeah? That was fantastic. Wow, I enjoyed that,' I said.

I hadn't seen a thing. The big moment had happened in the blink of an eye and my eye had been looking in the wrong place. The first pigeons home in Les's loft took a few gulps of water and a few pecks of corn, and then were out wandering about on the roof. 'Fuck me, 'ave you seen 'em?' said Les. He was excited.

'Look at 'em! Look at 'em! They look fuckin' tired.'

They looked all right to me. They were two very nice grey and white checker pigeons, heads bobbing as they walked around. They seemed to be moving pretty well. But what did I know? They had been flying for three hours or so, and if Les said they were tired then they must be tired. Pigeons regularly lose a substantial amount of their body weight when they fly, meaning they come home ounces lighter and needing to eat, drink and rest. 'Yeah, they look pretty knackered, Les.' But I don't think he heard what I said as his eyes were now locked on the sky once again.

'Some more here, Les,' said Pat, shortly after the first few came back. Pat was right, no seagulls this time, and when these pigeons appeared I actually managed to follow them back to the loft.

They came in a batch of five, flying low over the trees in front of the council estate, wings flapping rapidly. They hovered, circled and swirled above for a minute or two before finally swooping down into the loft in a whoosh of feathers, once again followed by Les and a now grinning Gary. It was all quite exciting, and was undoubtedly more so for the men in the loft trying to get the bands off

214

and into the capsules rather than for me standing outside the cabin staring at Pat while he rolled a cigarette.

By three-thirty p.m. thirty-five of the birds were back in the loft, although twenty were still missing in action. Gary and Les had stopped timing them in as the time wasn't important after the first dozen, but now they just wanted to see all the birds back safely. Pigeons sometimes don't make it back for one reason or another: being snatched by hawks, or flying into an electricity pylon are just two of the many possible reasons. 'They love being in the loft. It's their home so they'll be back,' said Les. 'At least they'll do what they can to get back.'

Les had more important things to think about now, like whether they had won first place and if the time of the first bird had been a good one. Les's times seemed to be much better than anyone on the phone had managed. It rang for the umpteenth time as I sat on the edge of the roof looking down on the sights of Oldham. Gary answered it. It was Gerry Clements from the Denton club, who was one of Les's main rivals in the federation. Les and Gerry didn't get on that well, and Les called Gerry the 'smiling assassin'. But there was professional respect between the two men, and the previous night

Gerry had complimented Les's pigeons before they were loaded into the transporter. He told Les he thought the pigeons 'were shining'. Les took the phone from Gary and minutes later he was punching the air.

'Whhhaaa fuckin' hoooooo!' Les shouted. 'I need a tea to celebrate. Put the fuckin' kettle on, Pat.'

Les's bird had beaten Gerry's bird by three or four minutes, although he didn't have the precise time as yet. The results would be worked out and compiled after the race and released the next day. But one thing was for sure, they knew they'd beaten Gerry. Gary smiled and joined me on the edge of the roof. 'At least we've beat Clements,' he said. 'It's very hard to predict where the winner will come from today, though. It could be us, you never know, but I think the wind will favour those further away. But at least we've beaten Clements.'

That seemed good enough for Gary, but once the excitement of beating Clements had died down I could see it wasn't good enough for Les. Les loved winning, after all. 'If we don't win I'm straight back home and I hardly speak all night. It's not really fair on the wife,' Les had said months earlier. 'But if we win it's 'get your glad rags on, we're going out' to the missus.'

216

When I walked back into the cabin it didn't look like Ruth would be slipping on the glad rags. By the look on Les's face, it seemed like a fish supper and last orders might be nearer the mark. Pat didn't seem overly concerned, though, as he dolloped a good helping of HP sauce on something unidentifiable on his plate. 'Hughes has come in before us. We haven't won,' said Les, looking serious. Losing wasn't a word he liked to use. 'Twenty seconds or so behind, we were. But the wind favoured him, I will say that. You can't win 'em all,' he added.

Les and the boys had been pipped to the post by a very good flyer from Rochdale called A. S. Hughes. 'He's a good lad him what beat us, though,' said Les generously as he came to terms with the result over the twentieth cup of tea. 'He tries hard and you can't win 'em all,' he said again before he stood up and added, 'I doubt anyone else has beat our time, though. I reckon we're still second, third, fourth and fifth. Can't see anyone else beating us.' Les's best bird of the day had in fact come in seventh, but the following week he had the first five places at a race from Cheltenham.

Les had counted them all out and by five p.m. he'd counted them all back in again. All fifty young pigeons were back in the loft, the

217

cocks and the hens as they had raced together. That's how it works with pigeons: the two sexes have equal rights, at least in racing anyway.

I hung around until the sun was fading and Gary was sprawled out on the bench in the cabin. 'At least we beat Clements,' he said again.

The race was over and the pigeons were wandering around on the roof of the loft. It didn't seem like the best time to raise the subject, but I had to speak to Les about the birds for South Africa before I left, and the clock was ticking. The pigeons had to be on the flight to South Africa in June, otherwise I'd be in the pigeon poop.

'So we're still on for South Africa then, Les?' I asked tentatively to ease my way in. Les looked preoccupied. 'South Africa?' he said. 'The birds for the race? Well, to be honest I can't send any.' He shut the loft door. 'I'm sorry, mate, but it's just too much. We've had a big order for pigeons over the past week and I just can't spare 'em. If I did send 'em I'd be losing money, and serious money at that. They are worth at least £500, each of those birds, and then I'm forking out £700 to send 'em. I can't do it, mate. I can't afford to lose that kind of money.'

Despite my pleading Les was unequivocal.

He'd had a change of heart and mine had just sunk a little. In desperation I thought of buying the birds off him but that wouldn't work. I'd be back to square one financially and more than likely banging on the door of the bookies and asking rascist Bill for his forgiveness.

'You don't want to buy 'em, mate. It's not worth it for that race. Like I say, it's a fuckin' lottery. You don't want to go shelling out thousands of pounds. That's crazy gear that. Listen, you've got a bit of time yet. Let me make a few phone calls and I'll see if someone can help you out with a few. There's bound to be someone who'll want to send some birds out there.'

As I walked down the rickety steps of Les's loft, the mad dog snarled and snapped its fangs, as if it had just been unleashed by the pigeon gods as a message to tell me that it was hopeless and that I shouldn't get involved with things I don't understand. This was becoming much more than a quest to join a pigeon race. As the dog leapt and gnashed, and I panicked and ran, it was almost as though this whole ridiculous episode was turning into a test of my courage, patience and endurance. A Homeric battle of wills, if you will. Me versus the pigeon gods.

'I'll bell a few people on Monday for yer?'

Les shouted as I left the warehouse. 'We'll get you a pigeon from somewhere.'

'Thanks, Les,' I said before walking into the evening sunshine towards the bus stop.

14

Bird Zero

'It's not pretty at all. They're, they're rats with wings . . . It's probably one of those killer pigeons . . . You see? It's got a swastika under its wings.'

Woody Allen, *Stardust Memories*

Amidst the pigeon love-in, while clasped in the bosom of pigeon reverie, I'd forgotten that the pigeon, in everyday life, is about as popular as a dose of the clap. In terms of its overall use, value and appeal, your average pigeon would probably gather fewer votes — in the great animal kingdom popularity contest — than the daddy-long-legs. In terms of its social status, the pigeon is probably more insect than bird. Birds are quite cute, and they sing and flit and float from tree to tree. The pigeon doesn't; it just flaps its wings, gets under your feet and bobs its head like a creepy clockwork toy in a granny's attic. Your average citizen squirms and turns their back rather than acknowledge the winged scruff pecking at the pavement. Apart from the racing fanatics only the very old, the very young and the fairly mad would squat down and offer the hand of friendship to the pigeon.

I was reminded of this as I walked outside the Tate Modern one sunny afternoon in late spring. I was having a break from pigeons and was looking for inspiration in my life; searching for a bit of meaning, some answers to some basic questions. What was it all about? Why had the pigeon invaded my life? The great surrealists of the twentieth century seemed a good place to start. But Dali and his mates let me down; I didn't find it in the gallery, I found it outside next to a tramp and an ice cream van.

The RSPB (Royal Society for the Protection of Birds) had pitched up with a stall, a telescope and three volunteers who were handing out leaflets. 'Would you like to look through the telescope?' one of them asked.

'Why?' I replied.

'There's a peregrine falcon on the roof of the Tate Modern.'

It was free and I had nothing better to do, so I looked through the telescope. But I couldn't see the falcon. It was like the Portland combine all over again. I didn't tell the woman I couldn't see it though.

'What did you think?'

'Very nice,' I said. The woman was friendly and she looked a bit like Judi Dench. She was apple-cheeked, with short hair and a posh voice, and she clearly liked birds, especially the peregrine falcon. 'What about pigeons?' I asked. 'What do you think of them?'

'Not much' her look said. She laughed nervously and inched away a bit. I think she thought I was a bit barmy and she was well within her rights to think that. Who cared about pigeons? No one, except my new mates and mad people.

'Well, we treat them as we do any other wild birds,' the woman straight-batted, while handing me a leaflet and edging back to the stall selling cuddly peregrine falcons. 'A few too many of them about though.'

A few too many, eh? And you're representing a bird lovers' organization. I was going to go for the jugular and expose the hypocrisy. 'You'd kill the pigeon, would you, and the racing pigeon as well? They are one and the same, are they?' I thought I sounded like Jeremy Paxman, jumping down the throat of Jack Straw on the issue of weapons in Iraq. But I realized people were now staring so I skulked off.

Why was I getting so worked up? What did I care? But I discovered that I did actually care, a bit at any rate, at least about the racing pigeon, which in the eyes of the RSPB and practically everyone else was classified in the same crummy group as the feral pigeon. They were both the chavs of the bird world in the eyes of most people. The racing pigeon's attempts at upward mobility in the social sense had not been noticed. If the street bird suffered then so did the winged wonder. Was the pigeon really that bad? And was the rough treatment of the pigeon warranted? It seemed like no one cared.

Les's friend Albert cared — about the racing pigeon, at any rate — and he thought the pigeon was getting a raw deal. Albert was the man who'd sent a letter of complaint to the *Manchester Evening News* about the use of hawks to cut down on pigeon numbers in the town centre. 'All the 'awks do is 'ave our fuckin' pigeons. 'Awks don't do any good to stop pigeons roaming the streets,' Albert had said.

Albert wasn't alone with his views on hawks. There were complaints about the cost and effectiveness of using hawks in this way in Trafalgar Square and other tourist parts of London where pigeons were a problem. Ken Livingstone, who wasn't a fan of the pigeon (he called it the 'flying rat' — very original, Ken), had been flying Harris hawks around

Trafalgar Square for some time as part of a crackdown on pigeons.

The mayor saw fit to ban the pigeon-seed seller in the Square in 2002 and threatened to impose £50 fines on anyone caught feeding the birds. The hawks were employed to patrol the area in case the pigeons found food elsewhere. That was the idea, but someone had worked out that the hawks were costing the London taxpayer £1,780 for each of the 121 pigeons killed a year, and weren't even that effective. The total Harris hawk bill for the taxpayer was £215,375, plus £30,000 to check if the feeding programme — to take away the pigeon food supply — was still working. Ken's people countered: 'Droppings cost £140,000 a year in damage to Nelson's Column and the Square, as well as being a nuisance and a health hazard.'

So, what was the problem with pigeons? Why all the fuss? I rang the environmental department of Manchester council to see if they could enlighten me. 'Bird droppings,' came the curt reply from a man called James. Like the mayor of London and his team, James was going in hard on the droppings argument. 'Bird droppings are unsightly, and their acid corrodes stonework and damages buildings. Droppings on pavements can make the pavements slippery and cause accidents.

They can also block guttering, as can nest materials and dead birds, consequently causing water damage to buildings. A dead bird in an uncovered tank can also contaminate the water supply. You wouldn't want a dead bird in your water tank, would you?'

I certainly wouldn't. But he didn't stop there. 'Pigeons can also carry a range of diseases such as salmonella and tuberculosis. It hasn't been proved that they can pass these on to humans, but there is always an outside chance. The droppings can also contain a variety of mites and insects that can cause skin irritations or allergic reactions. On the whole it's better not to have them around.'

Crikey! On the pigeon poo issue James seemed like he had a strong argument, and Albert's position was weakening the more I thought about it. Losing the odd racing pigeon was nothing to the spread of disease and blocked gutterings, surely? But Albert didn't think so and he wasn't the only one fighting the pigeon's corner. There were several other protesters in the wings and Julia Fletcher was one of them.

Julia was the leader of the Pigeon Action Group, a splinter faction of the once formidable Pigeon Alliance, a group of animal rights activists who got together to oppose Ken Livingtone's crackdown on pigeons in Trafalgar Square. 'There is no evidence to say that pigeons pass on diseases to humans. It is propaganda to cover up the greatest wildlife cruelty catastrophe London has ever known,' said Julia from her base in Cambridge.

'It's disgusting what is happening to these birds. Livingstone's office are starving huge numbers of the flock to death and the RSPCA are doing nothing about it. If I were to carry out some of the terrible atrocities that are being carried out on the pigeon on any other animal, I would be arrested,' she continued angrily. She didn't like Ken Livingstone or the RSPCA and, to be honest, she didn't like pigeon racing much either. In fact she thought it was an abomination.

'It's horrendous,' she said. 'I'm against using animals for the entertainment of others.'

I had to put Julia straight on this one. Entertainment? I'd take her to the next Portland combine race and see if she thought it was entertainment. 'But pigeon men love their birds. Some of them love their pigeons more than their wife and kids,' I tried to reason.

'The birds are taken away from their mothers as eggs and are made to fly for sport. It's cruel. It's terrible,' she said. There was no telling Julia.

Niel Hanson was another in the trenches with the pigeons. Niel was the spokesman for another splinter group — the Save the Trafalgar Square Pigeons organization. It was a mouthful but at least there was no room for ambiguity. Niel's organization, so he said, 'was a much bigger group than Julia's' and they had at least talked with the mayor's office about the problem.

'Julia? I wouldn't call them an organization. They are just a couple of people who feed the pigeons in the afternoon,' said Niel dismissively on the phone. 'We've got a lot of people who are actively feeding on a day-to-day basis and a few hundred people up and down the country who are on the mailing list as supporters.'

'How many active members have you got in total?' I asked.

'Probably a dozen or so who are active and go out feeding and so on.'

'How many people out there now?'

'Two people a day.'

Niel, like Julia, opposed the mayor's plans to reduce pigeon numbers. Niel thought the birds gave people a lot of enjoyment and had been there for generations. Surely after all these years they had some kind of squatters' rights?

'If the pigeons were doing any great harm

in terms of disease, I think we would have noticed by now,' he argued. 'Back in 2000 the House of Lords asked for a report from the government's chief veterinary officer to find out if the birds presented any health problems. He came back and said they didn't. We've consulted a vet called David Taylor and he said that in his fifty years of professional practice he has never seen anybody who has been infected by a pigeon. And it's particularly cynical of the mayor to keep talking about avian flu in the context of pigeons in Trafalgar Square, because pigeons are actually resistant to avian flu.'

So what did he think was Ken's beef with the pigeons?

'He's opportunistic, and uses any argument he can, like avian flu. We have been told by an official quite close to him that he has got a phobia of pigeons and that that's really what the issue is about, and that's why he has dedicated so much time and energy to getting rid of them.'

Ken Livingstone is scared of pigeons. Is that what it's all about? I needed a more objective view from someone who neither loved nor hated the *Columba livia*.

'I know someone who's in the pigeon business,' said my girlfriend one night as I passed the After Eight mints. 'I think he exterminates them,' she added. 'He used to have a car with the number plate 'Bird Zero'.'

A pigeon exterminator? An image of a man in a jump suit with a flame thrower and a wild look in his eyes came to mind. Then that image faded and I had a face something more like Lee Harvey Oswald's: unshaven, desperate and sweating as he looked down the barrel of his rifle before administering the perfect shot. The pigeon assassin. Maybe not the objective character I was looking for, but what did I have to lose?

Gary was the bird control specialist for one of the largest pest control organizations in the UK — he didn't 'deal with rats or mice, just birds' — and to my great disappointment he was nothing like Lee Harvey Oswald and didn't carry a flame-thrower. He was a nice family man who supported Nottingham Forest and played golf. 'I actually quite like pigeons and tend to dissuade people from killing them because it doesn't work,' said Gary matter-of-factly. Gary's company was a member of the RSPB and they thought the key to controlling pigeon numbers was keeping the streets clean from food.

'I generally work in urban environments and I don't have control of the food source. If you don't have control of the food source, killing the birds by shooting or trapping them, or using narcotics, isn't going to work as a means of controlling the numbers. Killing them is expensive and it doesn't achieve what my clients want. Most of my clients are banks, retailers or large developers and what they want are buildings and fire escapes free from bird fouling.'

The bird control business was worth around £15 million a year in Britain and Gary was very aware that ethical practices were more in tune with twenty-first-century business. Because he thought killing birds wasn't the way forward he used a whole range of other methods, including proofing: 'If you go to any tall store building and look up you will see tension netting, drop netting. Systems you put on ledges and roofs to stop birds landing.'

Gary had some great methods of scaring away unwanted birds. 'You can use distress calls, ultrasonics, predator-eye balloons, plastic hawks, plastic owls, all sorts,' said Gary, before moving on to a description of a wonderful-sounding contraption called the daddy-long-legs. 'The daddy-long-legs are upside down arms that wave around. But in most cases they won't work, not against pigeons. There was a case of a company who was developing flats in Birmingham — millions of pounds' worth of property and they bought fifteen plastic owls from us. I said, 'We'll supply them but they won't work.' So they are selling apartments for three or four hundred thousand pounds and on the ledge is a plastic owl. Our surveyor drove past and there was one pigeon sat on its head and about five sat fouling around it.'

I guessed that it didn't really matter what methods you used. The pigeon was a tough old bird and one that would always find a way to forage a living. It would always be hanging around somewhere in great numbers. Pigeons had been around since Moses, defied Ghengis Khan, Napoleon and the Luftwaffe so it was unlikely that Ken Livingstone or a plastic owl was going to do much to dent the numbers. So after all that, were they such a health hazard? Were pigeons really that bad?

'There are occasions when people get diseases from birds, but these are very rare,' said Gary. 'It's like bird flu: you have to be in there, involved in the removal of fouling or with poultry, to be at risk in any way. The problem isn't the pigeon, it's just where it drops its waste. At the end of the day, it smells and it's disgusting and people don't like it.'

15

Don't count your pigeons

'The human bird shall take his first flight, filling the world with amazement, all writings with his fame, and bringing eternal glory to the nest whence he sprang.'

Leonardo da Vinci

Paul Smith had already made one shipment of several hundred pigeons from the UK to South Africa in May 2006 — they didn't fly on their own, of course; they were boxed up and sent by a company called Hellman Worldwide (who are experts in pigeon freighting) from Heathrow to Johannesburg — and the final shipment at the end of June was looming. Hellman was waiting.

'Because of bird flu the pigeons will have to spend a week or two more in quarantine,' Paul had told me. 'So you'll have to get a move on . . . if you know what I mean.'

I was running out of time. I needed three pigeons for that final shipment and it would cost me nigh on £700 when all the shipping and medical costs were lumped on top. But I'd have to find the money, or a business partner, or both. Somebody with three good pigeons, that's all I needed, preferably ones with a chance of winning, and somebody who wouldn't get too angry if the birds were lost or eaten by a snake.

Les had made his intentions clear. He didn't want anything to do with the South African race and, after the disappointment and the dust had settled, I understood why. It was an expensive risk — he was right — and one Les couldn't afford (and didn't need) to take with his pigeons as his reputation in the business was built on winning. What was the point of paying to send birds to a race if you only had a 1000/1 chance of coming out on top? They weren't the odds a clever punter usually fancied. 'I don't want to knock it,' said Les, 'but it's not our type of racing. The distance and the training of the birds is not our thing. But you go for it. The money's there to be won and a lot of fanciers are into it. You'll find someone.' I hoped I would. I'd come this far, and I didn't want to go skulking out of the pigeon loft without at least seeing a bird with my name on it flap its little wings in the South African sunshine.

Frank said he knew someone. He called to say that Steve 'the oracle' was keen to speak to me now he'd inherited what was left of Moonie's loft. 'You know what Steve's like, he can lend his hand to anything,' said Frank.

I did know what Steve was like and basically I couldn't have thought of a worse person to join forces with. As much as I liked Steve — he had great lock-ins and he kept his ale pumps clean — he was a know-all at the best of times, and if he had an advantage of more knowledge than you on any subject, as he might have had with me on pigeons, he would be all over you like a cheap lampshade. He would leave you numb with his self-proclaimed expertise, before finally suffocating you with his conspiracy theories and leaving you lying in a heap with a head full of misinformation.

'Colin Powell's dad played for Celtic,' was one of Steve's late-night favourites.

'No, that was Gil Scott Heron's dad.'

'Who? No it was Colin Powell. No doubt about it. I read it the other day. Did you know that the drummer from Slade proposed to Rose West? How different it could have been if she had married the bloke from Slade,' he would say. Indeed.

Steve was a diamond in many ways, but he was basically confused and a bit of a reactionary. Something like a cross between Alf Garnett and the character that Harry

Enfield created, who was always hanging over your shoulder saying, 'You don't want to do it like that.' I could hear Steve behind me at the South African loft and imagine his big sweating face reddened by the sun. No, Steve was out of the question and anyway, to be fair, Moonie's birds weren't of the right age or quality anyhow.

I mulled it over for several days and then, as I was on the verge of having second thoughts and ringing Steve, it came to me: Bobby Rimmer. Who could be better to replace Les than Bobby Rimmer, aka 'Kid Dynamite'?

Bobby was the man who had introduced me to Les way back at the start of all this pigeon carry-on. Bobby 'Kid Dynamite' Rimmer was an ex-boxer from Gorton (although he wasn't a kid any more; he was in his forties and a bit overweight) and a keen pigeon racer of note. Bobby used to train the world light welterweight champion Ricky and he kept and flew pigeons from a loft above the gym where Hatton trained in a converted hat factory in Denton, Manchester.

Bobby had split with Hatton's camp and had been out of boxing for several months. He was running a pub but he had a bit of time on his hands and was game for anything. He was the perfect candidate. He also had good pigeons, many of them bought directly from Les, so on the whole it was the next best thing to having the man himself. There was a good chance the pigeons would still have that Les Green swagger and Salford spirit. I rang Bobby.

'I'll 'ave some of that,' said Bobby enthusiastically. 'It'll be a good crack and it'll test the pigeons. I've got three here in the loft ready to send.'

'We need them by the twenty-first of June,' I told Bobby.

'No problem, mate,' replied Kid Dynamite.

Bobby had saved the day, or so I thought. I celebrated with a cup of tea and a Jammy Dodger. I knew how to live. The pressure was off: I was going to send Les's pigeons after all and I didn't even have to pay Les prices. Bobby and I would split the costs of the entry and shipping, so it seemed to be the perfect solution; the big one was back on. Halleluja the missiles were flying! I smiled a satisfied smile and the Dodger got too soggy and fell in the tea. Was it a sign? Was the broken Dodger in the tea a portent of what was to come? I'd made a childish error and forgotten the famous old proverb: 'Don't count your pigeons before they're flying.'

My reprieve had been short lived because Bobby went awol. His enthusiasm for the race had also been short lived. Very short. Practically the day after we'd agreed on the phone to send his pigeons Bobby disappeared, and for the next few weeks he existed only as a broad Mancunian voicemail message: 'Sorreh I can't take your call at the moment . . .' And a week before the pigeons were due to be shipped he still hadn't materialized. Just seven more days and that would be it, the dream would be over. I'd have to wait another year and could I be arsed? No, was the short answer to that.

I rang Les in desperation. Maybe he'd seen Bobby. 'Nahh,' said Les. 'He does that from time to time. He just fucks off.' That wasn't the answer I'd wanted to hear but then Les threw me a lifeline.

'Listen. I may know one or two people who can help yer. Why don't you go and see Andy and his mate Stuart in Chelmsford? They're a couple of good lads and very good flyers. Can't promise anything but they might be able to see you right.'

I'd run out of options so I was on the train to Chelmsford the day after.

★ ★ ★

''Ave you ever handled a ferret?' asked Andy. I would have been lying if I'd said that I had.

238

'Or smelt a polecat?'

Again I couldn't admit to that.

'No, and I don't really . . . ' I was going to say 'want to', but it was too late. I had a ferret on my chest, I could smell its hot breath — a faint whiff of musk and old peanuts — and its glowing pink eyes were inches from my chin, along with its razor-sharp teeth and its ridiculously long and vicious-looking claws.

'Stinks, doesn't he?' said Andy, grinning. 'He's a beauty, though. He's the best I've ever had and he's so strong. He bit him in there,' he said, pointing to another evil-looking ferret in the cage. 'Don't ask me why he did it. I don't know.'

'He is a beauty, Andy,' I said. I smiled and didn't move much until Andy had grabbed the ferret by the scruff of the neck and stuck him back in his cage. 'Can I have a look at your pigeons now?' I asked.

Andy Jiggins kept his small team of birds, about thirty or so, in a pigeon loft he had built himself at the back of his handsome little bungalow, just outside Chelmsford in the Essex countryside. He walked me proudly into his widowhood loft, where the hens waited to tease the cocks. 'You can see the passion in that little pigeon,' Andy said, pointing to a checker hen. 'It doesn't look like much, but after a while they get hold of yer.

There is a bond. That's the passion between man and pigeon. That's what can happen. Then you can get the nicest and most beautiful-shaped pigeon in the world and you're handling it thinking, 'This can't be beat,' and it's a complete and utter duffer. But that's life. The pigeon's no good and you can't explain why. That's life isn't it?'

We left the widowhood loft and entered another section. 'Did Les show you the young 'uns?' Andy asked as we walked. The loft was bigger than it had looked outside. There were three parts to it; it was like an untidy pigeon-filled Tardis.

'Ugly little buggers, aren't they,' he said fondly, plonking a very hot ball of pink pigeon flesh and wispy grey feathers into my palm. The tiny pigeon sat on my hand breathing. It couldn't do much else. Andy smiled, but the mother of the pigeon didn't look too pleased. She flapped her wings and began to move threateningly.

'That's only two days old. Lovely little thing innet. People don't realize how beautiful these birds grow up to be.'

'Yes,' I replied, handing him back the squab. 'I think we'd better go.' I didn't want to get caught up in a Hitchcock-style bird attack so I edged towards the door until Andy followed me out. 'They won't do anything,' said Andy. 'Pigeons are the most gentle birds in the world.'

Andy had lived in Essex all his life, in one place or another, although his accent was softened with a slight hint of countrified Suffolk. He said 'innet' instead of 'innit', and sometimes finished a sentence with 'me boiy'.

Like many of the men I'd met recently, Andy had got the pigeon bug from his father as a youngster, and his surroundings — miles of open fields — had encouraged it further. Andy was an outdoors man and a dab hand at minor field sports. As well as pigeons he loved trapping, ferreting and shooting. He was big and heavy set, with thick forearms and huge hands. He'd made his living in the building trade and through various other physical endeavours, and despite the soft edge to his accent the broad, scarred nose hinted at Andy's past penchant for a fight.

'He was a bit of a boy in his day,' Les had told me. As far as I could see he was still a bit of a boy. Andy was in his late fifties or thereabouts, but he had a youthful bounciness about him, and a rascal's grin was never far from his face. Andy's house was surrounded by fields of bright yellow oilseed rape and as we walked out of his loft he stopped for a moment, opened the gate at the back of the garden, pointing to a spot next to the field. 'See where that stick is over there? There's about six rabbits up there,' he said, that grin spreading across his weathered face. 'In the winter I'll go up there with the ferrets and I'll 'ave that lot. They're all my dinners, they are.'

Andy was a good pigeon man. He'd won his share of races and he was up at half past five most mornings to feed and water his birds, trying his best to balance a passion for pigeons with a full-time job. But Andy also had another country-based passion. There was one minor field sport — if you could call it a sport — that he loved more than any other, and that was poaching. In his youth Andy had been the scourge of the local gamekeeping fraternity with his nocturnal activities.

'Oh, I loved it. What a buzz,' he said as we walked back to his house. 'Haven't been for some time but I could take you if you want, me boiy. But you'd 'ave to be able to carry a bunch of pheasants and they're 'eavy, they are. 'Ave you ever carried ten pheasants?' Again I couldn't say in all honesty that I had. 'Bloody 'eavy they are,' Andy repeated.

Andy had enjoyed those dark nights crouched in the undergrowth with his sights set on a big pheasant. He would often go out alone, or sometimes with his mate Hairy

Dave, bag a few pheasants and give them away to the locals. 'I'd never sell anything. It wasn't about that. Anything I got I'd give to people in the village.'

As we walked back to the house I asked him what it was about, the poaching malarkey. 'Well, people did it to eat, obviously, but for me it was just part of who I was and where I grew up. Being so close to nature an' all that. It was just something you did. You never really thought about it. But it was great though, a great buzz. One night three of us went out and we were all drunk,' said Andy, barely able to contain his laughter as he summoned up the memory. 'We were full of beer and me mate came across one of the gamekeepers.'

In a panic, on bumping into the custodian of the countryside, Andy's pal tried to fire off a shot into the night. 'God's honest truth he's gone click and it was empty, but we run. Anyway, Hairy Dave is behind us and all we can hear is him throwing up 'cause he wasn't used to the beer, so we stop 'cause none of us can run any further and Hairy Dave is saying, 'Can I stop for a bit? Me feet are killing me.' We'd gone for miles. My other mate says, 'Don't you think that our feet aren't hurting?' Hairy Dave says, 'Yeah, but I've lost me shoes and socks.''

Andy laughed loudly at the thought of Hairy Dave running barefoot through the night and so did I, even though I'd never met Hairy Dave. 'Might take you up there sometime if you fancy it,' he added when he'd stopped laughing. I smiled and remained silent.

★ ★ ★

Stuart Elvin was, according to Andy, 'the best pigeon sprint racer in Essex'. And he was right. I checked and Stuart had won numerous federation and combine prizes since he first started flying pigeons in the early sixties, and his reputation as a dedicated flyer and an all-round decent bloke had gained him the presidency of the Essex Central Federation.

'The worst advisor we've ever 'ad,' said Andy as he introduced me to Stuart.

'Yeah, but I make very quick decisions,' said Stuart.

'Very quick, but all the wrong ones,' Andy countered.

Andy and Stuart had been friends and rivals for years. Stuart was smaller than Andy but talked quickly, sometimes out of the side of his mouth, and with a machine gun-type delivery, like a cockney James Cagney. When it came to pigeons, Stuart had the energy of a man half his age. He was up out of his seat and shouting when he talked about pigeons.

'I paid twenty-five quid for a pigeon in 1961 — a Billy Ferris pigeon which had won a helluva lot — and that was like six weeks' wages for me. That made me, that pigeon did. And my father told me to do it. He said, 'You won't get any trouble off these pigeon racers round here. They're frightened of you round here. You're too keen for them and they're frightened of your keenness.' I was round everyone's house back then asking, 'How do you do this?' and 'How do you do that?' and watchin', and I'm pretty quick on the uptake, I am, I don't miss much, and then when you get a little bit clever, when you start to learn the game, they all say, 'You don't want to help this bloke, he's too dangerous.''

They were something of a double act, Jiggins and Elvin. More Cannon and Ball than Morecambe and Wise, but they were pretty good all the same.

'There was a punch-up in our club the other week. A seventy-year-old against a fifty-two-year-old cripple,' said Stuart.

'Fighting with pigeon baskets,' added Andy. 'Over nothing it was. Just a couple of firebrands these two old boys. One of 'em can hardly walk and the other one's only got half

245

a brain. But that's typical. You get all sorts in pigeons.'

'The seventy-year-old has got a moped,' said Andy, 'and he came in the other night with his helmet on. I said, 'You'd better keep that on; you never know what might happen in 'ere.''

Andy disappeared and came back with an enormous bottle of German hock. 'Only two pound thirty-eight this,' said Andy. It was going to be one of those nights. The glasses were filled and as the hock went down I started trying to convince them to compete in the Million Dollar race.

'I think Les has some issues with a few of the people that run the race,' Stuart said. 'That's why he won't enter any birds. And I'm not sure whether I would want to if I'm honest with ya.'

The shorter distances suited Stuart's pigeons and that's the way he liked it. He wasn't at all keen on the longer-distance races like the Sun City.

'I entered a few years ago,' he said. 'We had three in the race. The blokes down the pub all chipped in to pay the £700 or so but the birds didn't come anywhere. They got home, just about, that's the best I can say.'

The hock went down well, probably a bit too well, and as the evening sun dipped behind the trees outside I began to forget why I was there. Stuart and Andy were reminiscing about a pigeon-racing friend of theirs — an octogenarian ex-safecracker called Pat Mullan who kept an assortment of wildlife in his front room.

'He's one of the real colourful old-timers, is Pat. He would 'ave helped you out,' said Stuart. 'He had a van once; and he used to cart pigs around in it. He tipped it over once 'cause he'd overloaded it with hay. You'd never seen anything like Pat Mullan's house. We thought he had a mohair carpet but it was the dog 'airs. The foxes were in a baby pen in the front room. I went in there and he says, 'I bet David Attenborough would like to see these.' He had a video camera and he filmed them growing up. They used to keep him up all night, 'cause they're nocturnal. But he's a lovely bloke, Pat. Would help anyone. If he was still racing he'd be up for joining up with yer. Pat would have had a crack at the Million Dollar race.'

Pat might have been a contender, if he hadn't been eighty and ready for an old people's home. 'I pity the home that gets him. He'll drive 'em mad,' said Stuart.

Andy wasn't up for the race either, and not even another bottle of hock could persuade him. 'I've just sent three pigeons to the

Europa race in Cardiff so I can't afford to send any more. £30,000 first prize, that is. I'll be all right if that comes in,' he said as he poured me another large glassful.

It's over, I thought. The dream is over. As I stared out across the lush Essex landscape outside and gulped down the hock, I resigned myself to the inevitable. At least I'd tried and better men than me wouldn't have got this far — from Oldham to Chelmsford and back. Not bad; it was no disgrace. I drank more wine before I said my goodbyes to my new friends, and I sat on the train taking large gulps from another bottle that Andy had kindly given me before I left. 'It's only £2.38 and I've got loads,' he'd said before I staggered onto the train.

When I'd recovered, I rang Paul Smith. It was the day before he was to send his final shipment of pigeons to South Africa, and I told him that I wasn't going to make the deadline. Les didn't want in and I couldn't find anyone else. Paul listened to my problem before coming up with a well-considered answer.

'If you can't send any now a small number come on sale in January on the internet. Anyone can buy them, but it's first come first served. It's the same price — $1,000 for three. Or if you don't want to do that, you can join one of my syndicates. I normally have a few running. You won't win the full amount but you'll be competing, you'll be in the race. Let me know if you want to do it.'

I told him I would think about it, but before the phone had settled back in its cradle I already knew what my answer would be.

16

The Syndicate

August

OFFICIAL SHARE CERTIFICATE

for the

PAUL SMITH SYNDICATE

These are the full details of the 36 pigeons that were sent out to represent this syndicate:

Blue Hen — Wonderwoman
Blue Cock — Wonderman
Blue Ch. Hen — Superstar
Blu Ch. Hen — Lightning
Blue Ch. Hen — Express
Blue Cock — Rocket
Blue Hen — Millionairess
Blue Hen — Million Dollar Baby
Blue Ch. Cock — Navigator
Blue Ch. Hen — Something Special
Blue Hen — Something Gold
Blue Cock — Luckything
Blue Hen — Claudia

Blue Hen — Lady Diana
Blue Ch. Cock — Sundowner
Dark Ch. Hen — Jackpot
Blue Cock — Pot of Gold
Blue Ch. Hen — Heartcrusher
Blue Hen — Wondergirl
Blue Ch. Hen — Supergirl
Blue Ch. Cock — Superman
Blue Ch. Cock — Hurricane
Dark Ch. Cock — Blockbuster
Blue Cock — Concorde
Blue Hen — Millionaire
Blue Ch. Cock — Terminator
Blue Cock — Prospector
Blue Ch. Hen — Luckycharm
Blue Ch. Hen — Something Super
Blue Ch. Cock — Luckybird
Blue Hen — Natalie
Blue Hen — Sundancer
Blue Ch. Hen — Sun City
Blue Hen — Hit the Jackpot
Blue Ch. Hen — Heartbreaker
Blue Ch. Cock — Heartbroken

£228 sterling bought me a share in the Paul Smith syndicate and for that tidy sum I became part owner of the thirty-six pigeons sent to the Sun City Million Dollar pigeon race 2007. The names were lousy but who cared? Certainly not the pigeons.

251

£228 gave me thirty-six chances at the big prize. It seemed fair enough considering the choice I faced: join the syndicate or forget the race. So I paid it. I'd had enough of all the messing around. All the train journeys and telephone calls, chasing pigeons, chasing Les and chasing shadows. I'd have to share the money with a few other people if I won. Exactly how many I wasn't too sure at that point. But it was fine by me. We might get two or three birds in the top positions anyhow. Who could say how many of the thirty-six winged wonders would figure in the reckoning? And then there'd be lolly for us all. I was feeling optimistic — stupidly so.

All the pigeons at the loft in South Africa, once released from quarantine, were put through a pretty rigorous training regime. There were unofficial training flights every week, official training flights every other week — each around 80 km — and five races over longer distances — between 200 km and 400 km — they called 'Hot Spots'.

As a shareholder I had a chance to win a portion of any of the prizes won but I wasn't holding my breath. After all, I kept being told that the races were more about the conditioning of the birds than the booty. The Hot Spots were designed to sharpen up and acclimatize the birds and sort out the wheat from the chaff. Hundreds of pigeons were lost in those training flights every year. There were some that just couldn't hack the weather and the ever-looming threat of the predators and as a shareholder I received regular updates from Paul, meticulously detailed, to let me know if any of the syndicate's pigeons had been lost in the wilds of Africa or eaten by something or other. Not that Paul actually knew whether they'd been eaten or not — the reports weren't that meticulous.

September

GOOD NEWS

for shareholders in the

PAUL SMITH SYNDICATE

This syndicate originally entered 36 pigeons, and lost three around the lofts before training started and then another one on the first training flight. That resulted in 32 going into the second training flight and all 32 returned, meaning that all 32 in the loft have flown on the training tosses so far.

No car and no money, but at least no MIA — apart from the ones who were lost before it even started. But they didn't count, useless toerags. We still had thirty-two feathered wonders going strong, and that was no small victory — what with the weather and the snakes, we were two training flights down and nearly a full squadron still intact. Not bad at all.

Les Green and the team had also had some good news as the 2006 season drew to a close. As usual they'd come out on top in the Oldham Federation — thirty-seven first prizes — and despite the disruptions caused by bird flu, they'd also had a relatively successful season financially. 'The Ferrari's still on hold, but we've not done bad at all this year, as it goes,' said Les. 'Can't fuckin' complain at all.'

Unfortunately the late-summer winds of good fortune and prosperity weren't warmly caressing the cockles of everyone in pigeon racing. The RPRA weren't having it so good. In fact at the end of the 2006 season the RPRA were facing up to a gloomy prospect akin to receiving the chill winds of winter through a hole in the seat of your trousers. Due to the restrictions imposed by DEFRA, the year had been a financial disaster. Membership and ring sales were down and they had lost £35,000 directly as a result of the sanctions. According to an RPRA press release, they were nearly £50,000 in the red and membership numbers were down by 6 per cent.

'2006 has been a nightmare for racing,' said Peter Bryant. 'Clubs were hoping to race from France and, despite the fact that racing pigeons pose a very low risk of catching or passing on bird flu (certainly no more than a human traipsing through an infected area), DEFRA declined to give us a licence to do so for very long. In fact they did not allow us to race our young birds from the continent at all, so August and September were a washout in that respect. If this is not addressed in 2007 then fanciers will not breed the usual number of pigeons, which will again affect one of our major income sources. Moreover, our membership numbers are down and this loss will certainly rise if we are not able to race a full season from France.'

December

INTERNATIONAL PRESS RELEASE

Saturday Training Flight Eleven

'What a Great Christmas present: a brand new motor is won by UK fanciers'

The United Kingdom team had another truly remarkable race . . .

Unfortunately our syndicate hadn't won the brand new motor, nor had a particularly remarkable race. Our highest place in the fourth Hot Spot race was 241st and we had only seventeen birds left as we approached the season of goodwill, which was a bit of a worry. Someone called Paul McCarthy from Merseyside had triumphed in the Hot Spot race. He was the lucky sod who won the motor — a Honda Civic — with a pigeon called Wallasey Jack. Good for him, and three cheers for Wallasey Jack. Our Paul told us not to worry though. 'The pigeons who do well in the Hot Spots rarely do anything in the final race,' Paul reassured me. Apparently there was no cause for concern — very good to hear.

The losses, although tragic in their own little way — Lady Diana and the Terminator were among the casualties — could also be recovered without too much fuss. Paul told me the syndicate had plenty of money in the pot to buy more pigeons once they became available in the January internet purchase window. Come the final shake-up we would have at least thirty birds in the race. It was still looking OK, at least as far as the numbers were concerned.

One major hurdle remained, however. Who was going to pay for my ridiculous excursion?

Before I forked out the money for the pigeons, I hadn't really given the booking of the trip much thought, preferring to adopt the blindly optimistic Mr Micawber 'something will turn up' approach.

I found out that Sun City wasn't cheap. In fact it was a bit pricey. It was after all the Vegas of the Rainbow Nation, the playground of the white South African, with ample gut and an even more ample wallet. The three hotels that accommodated the Sun City holiday complex were asking at least £150 a night. I'd been thinking more along the lines of forty pounds. Certainly not much more than the Savoy in Blackpool.

'You'd better get a move on,' reiterated Paul. 'The pigeon men usually book the place out and it's Chinese New Year.'

I didn't know what Chinese New Year had to do with it but all the rest was correct. I was in a spot of bother once again. I could see that I was turning into some kind of pigeon-chasing journalistic Frank Spencer, but without the acrobatics. Just the bad planning and execution of every dumb plan. I was in another seizure of panic and inwardly raging at the folly of my ways. Until my angelic new girlfriend slapped me around the mush and applied some good sense to the situation.

My new girlfriend Joanne worked on a newspaper that just happened to be angling for a story on a South African tourist site. Something had turned up and with it I got a flight and a room in a themed hotel in Sun City called the Palace of the Lost City. Look at me now, I'm on top of the world. Things are about to start happening.

January

GREAT NEWS

for shareholders in the

PAUL SMITH SYNDICATE

THE PAUL SMITH SYNDICATE originally entered 36 pigeons and we lost six prior to the first Hot Spot Race, so this meant that the syndicate actually had 30 fully paid-up pigeons flying for all prize money and awards in the race series. Since the first Hot Spot race this syndicate has lost another 14 pigeons; to be fair to all shareholders, I will now proceed as per the rules to purchase another 16 reserve pigeons to make our total again up to 30 in THE FINAL RACE.

Jimmy Richards was the man who had bred the thirty-six pigeons Paul had boxed up and sent to the Million Dollar race. Jimmy was seventy-one years old and had flown pigeons for over fifty years and, thankfully for us, he was one of the most experienced and well-respected fanciers on the circuit. I had to meet him.

'Jimmy's been an outstanding flyer over the years,' said Paul when I rang to ask him for Jimmy's number. 'And he's had great success both at home and in the Sun City race.'

Things were getting better. Did Jimmy train the pigeon that Paul had snaffled the $100,000 second prize with? 'No, that was from Hungary. But he's a very good pigeon man, is Jimmy. His birds are always competitive and have done well for us before.'

Jimmy and his birds, Paul told me, had won a National and several London combine titles and been placed in the top fifty at Sun City more than once. Jimmy also had a wealth of knowledge and was something of a sage when it came to pigeons.

'A bit like Yoda, I heard,' Frank had said. 'He knows pigeons.' I don't think Yoda knew pigeons, but I got what Frank meant — Jimmy was well known for being a mine of pigeon info. Fanciers went to Jimmy with their pigeon problems and he usually had the answers.

Jimmy lived half an hour outside London in a small town called Laindon in Essex. When I arrived on a bright, crisp January morning he was waiting outside the station with a smile and a warm handshake. He was small and bald under his cap, and he had a finely wrinkled and friendly-looking face — there was something slightly Yoda-like about him.

'We'll 'ave a cup of tea and then go and 'ave a look at the loft, shall we?' asked Jimmy in a broad Essex accent as we took the short drive to his little semi-detached house.

Jimmy was, in his own words, an old-fashioned 'working-class pigeon man'. He was one of the old breed who had balanced pigeons with a job — at the Ford Motor works — rising at four or five in the morning each day to keep the birds in shape. 'I never made much money from pigeons,' he reflected as we sat drinking tea in his kitchen, 'but that's never been what it's about for me.' Jimmy said he wasn't a professional like Les, at least not in the sense that he worked full time on the pigeons. Jimmy had never seen it as a career move; he just did it for the love of it.

'Don't get me wrong, I love winning and

making a few quid. But I've done it for most of me life and I've never made a lot of money out of it. I get me state pension and me small pension from Ford's. I sell pigeons and do all right; I never 'ave to advertise, everyone knows who I am. But I don't make a lot out of it, just enough to buy what I need to keep me pigeons in good nick. But I think I have something more important than money: I have what is the most wonderful thing about pigeon racing and life: I have a lot of friends.' We finished our tea and Jimmy led me out to his back garden to show me his loft.

When it came to pigeons, Jimmy had friends in all sorts of high places and many of them thought nothing of giving him a few birds just to see if he could make them perform. Jimmy was something of a sounding board for other fanciers, especially the wealthy ones who wanted to test birds with no pedigrees. 'If anyone could make something out of nothing, Jimmy could,' was the general gist of it. Friends like the late Louis Massarella, who had set a British record for a pigeon purchase when he bought a bird for over £100,000 several years ago. 'He flew the pigeon over from Thailand and it had its own seat in business class,' I remember Les telling me.

Jimmy had around eighty pigeons in a loft

ingeniously crafted out of packaging from the Ford motor works. 'It was packaging sent over from America. Good stuff it was. Survived the hurricane it did,' he said, now sounding like Yoda as he smiled and pointed at the loft. 'Built it the year of the hurricane, 1987, and I lost just one tile.'

The pigeons in each section of his loft came in all colours and sizes. There were blue bars, blacks, checkers among others, and they all sat happily cooing in one section or another. They all had a calmness about them too, just like Jimmy.

'That's a winner; that's the mother of a National winner; that's another winner. Nothing but winners,' said Jimmy proudly.

'That's one of the sprinters; that's a widower hen; that's a son of Ebony Louise, the black hen who won the National; and these are cocks in here. I don't pair 'em up though. I let them do it natural,' he said with a wink as he led me into his breeding loft. Jimmy didn't think it helped the birds to force them together to mate. 'I let them pair up as they want to pair up. You don't take the mickey out of 'em; you let it happen naturally.'

Jimmy said the pigeons got upset when their youngsters had been reared and you separated them from the hens, which applied a similar technique to the widowhood system (the birds fly home to mate, but the cocks and hens are separated, with the hens being shown to the cocks just before a race). So you softened the blow as much as you could by helping to make the mating as stress-free as possible.

'It's a big upset when they are parted so you don't want to take the mick. They sulk — you'd be amazed, pigeons really do sulk. They sometimes even start crying.'

Most of the pigeons in Jimmy's loft had been bought for low prices — few had been bought for more than £200 — or had been handed down from 'friends' who saw Jimmy as a wise and reliable old head to try new stock out on. It was the loft of a man who knew how to make the best from limited resources.

'I bought one hen for thirty quid in a breeder buy,' said Jimmy, lifting up his cap and scratching his head. 'I bought it in 1999 and it came from Mr and Mrs Turner of Colchester from the red Daniel pigeons. I paired her with a pigeon called Nellie's Boy, and I've still got him in the loft now. He's seventeen years old and he's bred nothing but winners. Last year, the pigeon who was fortieth in South Africa was bred from it. So I put one in this year and I said to Paul, 'We've got to name this one something special.' And Paul, quick as a flash, says, 'That will be its name, Something Special.' And that's out there at the moment.'

'So, you think it has a chance, Something Special?' I asked.

'Well, you can't say for sure, but it's a good pigeon. There's no doubt about that. It's from good stock.

'A lot of very good fanciers are always sending me pigeons,' he continued. 'Sometimes once-in-a-lifetime pigeons to try out. I get a lot of new strains. Massarella used to send me down lots of different pigeons with no pedigrees 'cause it's good for them. I give 'em an honest appraisal and I tell 'em if I score with 'em or not, and it's free publicity for them as well.'

Publicity wasn't the only thing that benefited Jimmy's friends, however. Jimmy employed all kinds of little tricks and techniques that he'd picked up over the years to help him gain an edge, but he didn't feel it necessary to keep all his gems to himself. He'd 'mellowed' in his old age and wasn't afraid of passing the knowledge on to younger fanciers.

'You've got to keep people interested in this game. The numbers aren't what they were, so you've got to help where you can.

I've got young chaps your age in pigeons who think I'm God,' said Jimmy, matter of factly. 'Honest. I'm a silly old sod. When it comes to pigeons I don't know why, but they ring me up all the time. I don't know what it is. I just think I've got a feel for pigeons. I can't explain it. My old granddad used to have a farm in Essex, and maybe the stockmanship, having a feel for birds, just runs in the blood. I don't know. I call it luck, although it could be a gift; you can't really say.'

Jimmy gave the ambitious and enquiring fancier all kinds of tips from the little things like 'always give the birds bottled water; you don't know what crap the water board put in it these days,' to more loft-changing revelations such as: 'I went into this loft up north — a seventy-foot double-decker loft in a builder's yard — and the blokes had all the widowers there and I felt the loft was cold and I said to 'em I'd put straw on the floor which helps keep it nice and warm. They also had their pigeons loose in the loft. I always lock my widower cocks in the boxes 'cause all they can see is themselves, and it makes them a little more aggressive; they are very protective of that space, that domain. I also said, 'You've got all your nest bowls in the boxes, you need to take 'em out.' They said, 'Why?' So I said, 'I'll show you,' and I put the nest bowl on the floor and the pigeons went whoosh right into it and they said, 'Bloody hell you're a magician!' It's just a silly thing, hiding the nest bowl away and then Friday nights, as soon as you put that nest bowl in, they'll go barmy and that's good enough for them to win a race.'

As we left the loft Jimmy told me that the birds in South Africa were the 'best he could have sent', and all of them had been bred from winners. We went back into the house and he made me some bacon sandwiches. With Jimmy at the helm, things were beginning to look up.

January

GREAT NEWS

PAUL SMITH SYNDICATE

A staggering total of US $1.63 million dollars will be paid out in prize money to the top 250 pigeons in the 'Final Race', plus 10 gold medals and numerous trophies. All this equates to 'THE BIGGEST AND GREATEST ONE-LOFT PIGEON RACE IN THE WORLD TODAY.'

'You going to South Africa?' I asked Jimmy.

'Nahh,' he said. 'I can't afford it, but to be honest with yer I don't really like goin' away. Much prefer to stay here messin' about with the pigeons. I said to Paul, if we win, all I want is that green winner's jacket' — like the US Masters Golf Tournament, they have a green jacket for the winner — 'and the gold medal on my mantelpiece. That will do me. That will be lovely.'

'So what about the money?' I asked. 'What are you getting out of it financially, if you don't mind me asking?'

'Well, I have ten shares and the race doesn't cost me a penny,' he said as he sat down to eat his breakfast. 'I'm happy with ten shares and supposing we did go and win, I think we'd get $222,000. That would work out in my mind $22,000 for me. That's not bad, is it? And after the race the winning pigeons are sold and they bring in nice money. I get a percentage of that too, so that bumps the money up. I'm happy with it all. The Chinese and Taiwanese spend big bucks on pigeons over there. There are two Chinese ladies round here who buy pigeons for about fifty pounds each and then send them back over there and sell them for a hundred. And the Portuguese are the same. They're going bananas about pigeons in Portugal, they are, and also in Malta — it's very big in Malta.'

While Jimmy finished his bacon sandwich it suddenly dawned on me that maybe I wasn't going to get rich out of the syndicate. In fact it looked like I'd be lucky to even cover the bar bill. If Jimmy had ten shares and would only win $22,000 I would be looking at a grand sum of $2,000 if one of our pigeons came in first. I would have done better on a decent night at the Gala Bingo. $2,000? Not much for a year's struggle. What could I get for that? Half of a Koopman pigeon perhaps. £288 for one share — that didn't seem like the greatest deal I'd ever struck. But it was too late to complain now. My flight was booked and I was eating bacon sandwiches with the breeder and supplier.

'So how many people are in this syndicate?' I asked Jimmy. It was a question I should have asked Paul several months earlier, but I wouldn't have been involved in all this nonsense if I wasn't a bit of a cretin.

'Oh, about eighty, I believe,' Jimmy replied, stroking his Jack Russell terrier, Lucky.

Eighty? For crying out loud. By my reckoning that was around £20,000 in the syndicate pot. A whole lot of feathers.

'How many shares do you have?' Jimmy enquired.

'One,' I said.

'And how much did you pay for it, if you don't mind me asking?' said Jimmy.

'£288 quid.'

'Blimey,' said Jimmy as he removed our dirty plates from the table and dumped them in the sink. 'Let's hope we go on and win it then, eh?'

17

The Olympics of Pigeon Racing

'What an idiotic statement that we didn't vaccinate the pigeons. Why would we not spend 50p to protect an investment of £700? Are we that stupid? Clearly people would like to see the race fail for their own gratification and their own agenda. What they fail to realize is that the race is such a big event and so well liked worldwide that even if they get me out of a job, they are never going to kill the event.'

Zandy Meyer, race organizer

'It's a marathon,' Frank said as he wished me luck before I left for South Africa and the big race. 'The winner is the one that can stay the course. The one with the stamina.'

'Thanks, Frank,' I replied, not that I was running or flying the race myself. 'I'll remember that.' And off I went.

Sun City was built by the South African businessman Sol Kerzner in 1979, mainly for the discerning white South African who wished to shake off those Apartheid blues

270

with a game of golf and a night on the roulette wheel. The promotional pamphlet described it as 'a wilderness wonderland' — maybe not if you were one of the black menial workers — 'built into a volcanic valley and surrounded by the beautiful Pilanesberg mountains'.

Sun City pretty much consisted of four hotels, give or take a time-share, and Gary Player's golf course, which had hosted many of the best players in the world at one time or another. My hotel was the Palace of the Lost City. I'd lucked out. It was the grandest and most brazen of the lot.

'The palace? Bloody hell, I can't believe you're in there, I thought you were broke,' said Paul before I left. He sounded a little envious. Paul and most of the pigeon men were staying at a place called the Cascades hotel next to the Superbowl auditorium which hosted the pigeon people on race day.

'Not bad, is it?' I said.

'It's the most expensive hotel there,' Paul scoffed.

I didn't tell him I wasn't paying for it. For some reason I thought it might be better if he thought I wasn't just some dumb Okie who went around throwing money into pigeon syndicates. Not that he would have given it a moment's thought.

271

* * *

As the cab passed the checkpoint and drove up the winding road to the hotel I wasn't sure about 'wonderland' but Sun City, despite the dodgy political history, was not without its merits. The site employed many of the local black population, who probably had few opportunities to work in palatable environments, the rugged mountainous scenery was beautiful and the whole area was certainly an impressive feat of engineering. The hotels and the manmade lakes and beaches had been created in the middle of nowhere, proving that even the remote parts of Africa could be industrialized if there was a will and a tidy profit at stake.

The Palace of the Lost City was the jewel in Sun City's glitzy crown. It was themed around an ancient lost African civilization, apparently (it didn't specify which one) although it was 'guarded' by a life-sized bronze elephant and decorated with renaissance frescos, mosaic floors, ancient carvings and false tusks. It was five star luxury with access to an opulent Olympic-sized swimming pool — slightly more inviting than the one I used at the caravan site in Cleveleys as a kid — and the 'Shrine of the Sacred Monkey'. It was 'lit with the glow of a million candles' and, for one weekend only, filled to the renaissance frescos with fat pigeon racers from every cranny of the globe. Well, if you were going to go pigeon racing, why not do it in style? Maybe they should write that in the promotional brochure.

The Million Dollar pigeon race would climax on the Saturday afternoon in the Superbowl — an auditorium which seated 6,000 people and once hosted UB40 and Ronan Keating (not at the same time, though) — which was the centre piece of the Sun City entertainment centre.

I arrived on the Friday. There was no time to hang around — I needed to mingle and find some anwers to important questions. Who were the favourites? Did we have a chance? Had any more of Jimmy's pigeons been lost? I needed to find Paul.

Paul was in the Superbowl when I arrived, having been in Sun City for days. I looked terrible after the ten-hour flight, pale and tired, but Paul looked like a newborn baby, albeit a slightly wrinkly one with silver hair. Paul was glowing red, and garbed in pristine white shorts with a blue Great Britain pigeon racing shirt. He looked happy. This was his place. Paul got respect here and so he should. He'd overseen the basketing of 2,402 pigeons who were now on their way to the liberation point, in a transporter lorry, 552km (343 miles) away from the Sun City complex.

'You made it, then,' said Paul with a big grin on his face. He was talking to a group of what I could safely assume were pigeon racers. They were laughing about something or other, no doubt pigeon-related.

Apart from Paul and a small bald man, the men were all big and ample around the girth, some bigger than others, the biggest being a South African gent who was holding a can of beer, talking very loudly and swearing a lot. 'Do you think they train these pigeons and then come here and try not to try?' said the enormous South African. 'Do you think I'd send crap to this race?' rolling the 'r' with his tongue the way South Africans do. 'Do you think I'd send crrrap? You've got to be fucking kidding.'

A chubby man with silver hair looked around at his pigeon comrades, and then looked briefly at his white training shoes before taking a short breath and addressing the small crowd in an Antipodean accent. 'This is the hardest race track in the world,' he said. The men nodded in agreement. The South African took a big gulp from his can of beer. 'This is the Olympics of pigeon racing. The hardest race in the world,' he repeated. 'Of course they're fucking trying.'

Friday was billed as a 'day of leisure', a day to relax, have fun, check out the swimming pool, the shrine of the sacred monkey and the crocodile park, before the big race began in earnest early the next day. The birds were due to be liberated at six a.m. But talking pigeons was fun to the pigeon man. This was where he got his kicks. He didn't need sun, cool water and crocs to make him feel good. He didn't need to be draped on a sunlounger with a cocktail in hand, and a scorching African sun frying his ample gut. In the gloom of the Sun City entertainment centre debating the hot issues of the weekend, that was where the pigeon man got his jollies.

Paul called me over and introduced me to the men. They shook my hand and all seemed friendly now they'd got the business of pigeons not trying off their burly chests. Some of the names didn't register but the man with the silver hair and Antipodean accent was from New Zealand and his name was Ron. The smaller man was Ron's pal Colin, who was also from New Zealand, and the enormous South African was called Laurence.

'How are ya, mate?' said Ron. 'Are you a pigeon man yourself?'

'Not really,' I said.

'Well, you are this fuckin' weekend,' said

275

Laurence, grabbing my shoulder and laughing. 'You better get fuckin' used to it.'

The debates had been raging days before I arrived, I was told, in the bars around Sun City. The hottest issue was the health of the pigeons in the race. Nearly half the birds had been lost since the day they arrived in June 2006 and many people were asking why, including a Mexican pigeon racer who had lost more than most in the early stages. The Mexican had complained and then aired his grievances about the losses on a pigeon website, accusing the organizers of the Sun City race of, amongst other things, being corrupt and favouring pigeons from wealthier European countries such as Germany.

Zandy Meyer, the race organizer, hadn't been happy with the accusations and the Mexican pigeon man had been dismissed as a crank before a five million dollar lawsuit was flown his way to shut him up, but although his accusations had little or no hard evidence, in some respects he had a point.

With all things considered it looked to me as though the race was fair. Paul Smith, who vouched for Zandy and the race, was an honest man and the large numbers of pigeon racers who attended each year were testament to that. These weren't stupid people (not all, at any rate) and besides, it was almost impossible to favour one pigeon from another in the loft. Each bird had its identity tag covered with a tamperproof seal before entering the loft, so the loft manager, Dirk Engelbrecht, and his team had no chance of singling out one bird. It was a level playing field in that respect but there had been many losses before the 2007 race (over 2,000 in fact) and competitors had a right to know why. After all, it wasn't cheap to enter.

One theory doing the rounds of the entertainment centre, which the Mexican had suggested, was that the pigeons were sick. They had picked up a disease of some kind and that was why they were dropping like, erm, sick pigeons. All the birds had been vaccinated once they arrived in the loft, and some had been vaccinated before they were flown into South Africa, but even so some of the pigeon men at Sun City thought malaria was a possibility. Contracted in the loft from the dreaded pigeon fly. Laurence's friend Joe, who was stood, hands on hips, in the thick of the debate, thought it might be a possibility.

'I have nothing but admiration for this race,' said Joe in diplomatic fashion. 'But there must be something wrong and Zandy must look at it if this race is to get better. Malaria is rife here at this time of year. Most birds carry it. So what better than a loft full of pigeons?' Joe offered.

'Do you think, if these pigeons were sick, they would be where they are?' asked Laurence. 'If these pigeons are sick there is no way they would be where they are now, 3,000 kilometres down the line.'

Ron stepped in again. 'It's like I said before. This is the ultimate pigeon race. Of course you're going to get losses. This is the toughest race track in the world. These birds have to endure the weather, the predators and the distance. It's no wonder you get losses. But that's why we're here, isn't it fellas? To test ourselves against the best.' Everyone agreed with Ron. Either that or they were fed up with standing in the Superbowl arguing the toss. I certainly was. I was tired and in no state to carry on arguing without a good sit down.

Laurence finished his can of beer and suggested taking the pigeon chat into the bar. I joined them. I needed to get the inside track on the race and I had a gut feeling that these were the fellas who were going to give me just that. Laurence guided us to a place called the Rhino bar next to the casino. Which was appropriate — Laurence had a passing resemblance to a white rhino. He was, in true South African fashion, huge. His forearms were bigger than my waist and his mouth was bigger than my head.

'I played soccer for South Africa, I've just sold a huge business and I'm in the greatest race in the world. What does it matter if I'm overweight, or if I've lost my hair!' Laurence announced to the bar.

'There is nothing I can't do,' he said turning to me. 'Although this thing can kick you in the arse. You can go and be successful in pigeon racing and if you take your eye off the ball slightly and don't look after your loft you're in trouble. I'm fucking telling you, boy, it can kick you in the arse.'

Laurence was loud but he was generous. Certainly with the beer and the pigeon chat. Before I could thank him for the first bottle, another round of beers was standing to attention on the table in front of us, and Laurence was happily opening up a tab and settling in for a few more as afternoon turned into evening. It was Friday night in Blackpool all over again, only with hot weather and monkeys.

Ron, Colin, Laurence and Joe told me they had taken part in all of the South African Million Dollar races, and they all felt in with a chance.

'I don't fear anyone, not the Germans, the Belgians or the 'Poms'. I am here to win this race,' said Laurence emphatically. Ron and

Colin concurred. They had won everything there was to win in New Zealand, as far as pigeon racing went, and Laurence and Joe had big reputations in South Africa pigeon racing circles, especially Joe. Joe had what Laurence called a 'feather up his arse'.

'That's what I call a man who is pigeons through and through. He has a feather up his arse.' Joe smiled modestly and took a drink of his beer. 'I'm telling you,' Laurence continued, 'he's the only man who I allow to come into my loft to criticize. I won't let any fucker do that other than him. He is a pigeon man through and through and I trust what he says. If he says they are shit, then they are shit.'

Ron and Colin were also pigeon men through and through, although I wasn't sure if they had feathers up their arses. No matter, they were experts in their field. Ron especially so, as Colin preferred to sit quietly, smiling and glugging his beer.

'I'm trying to lead by example,' Ron told us. 'I've been twenty, thirty years in New Zealand as the national champion. I can't go any further than that. How can I go any further than that?' he asked, almost pleading with us. 'I can't get any better than that. So this is the international stage. This is where I need to test myself. When you can't go any further what do you do? I've been to

280

Bangkok. I've been to Korea and done exceptionally well there, I've bred birds and sent them to Germany and done very well in Germany. I've done well in Cardiff. The whole shooting box. So I'm not racing back at home now. Colin's racing back at home now.' Ron pointed to Colin. Colin smiled and glugged. 'And now Colin's winning everything. He's a top flyer now. So we are both stepping up, we are both on the international stage.'

Ron's best placing in the Million Dollar race had been eleventh and Laurence had been placed sixth in 2003. Colin's pigeons had been in the top fifty once or twice and Joe had been placed in the top 250 every year since the start but, he argued, with a smaller team of pigeons.

'People send numbers here. They send forty or fifty pigeons. You don't know how good someone is if they send forty or fifty pigeons. That's just all about numbers. Anyone can send fifty and get one home. That to me is not the way to do it. I send three or four pigeons. Now if you can send three or four and have them placed in the top 250 then you know you are on the right track in terms of what you select. Then you know you are selecting well, and that to me is the secret of pigeon racing, the selection.'

Joe reckoned he could see a bird was going to be a winner right from the egg. Joe was something of a pigeon mystic. He had an uncanny feeling for a good pigeon as well as a bad one.

'He's a fuckin' genius, this boy,' Laurence confirmed.

'You can see it from the egg?'

'If you know what to look for you can see it virtually from the day the egg is laid,' Joe said. 'You know that eggshell quality is a direct reflection of the strength of the bone. The bone structure must be very strong. You will see when I handle pigeons. I first touch the back and then I touch the right wing. And if I touch the back and I don't like it I won't look any further. The pigeon has a weak side, did you know that?'

'No,' I admitted. The rest of the table nodded.

'Many people don't know that. Like in humans you can be strong with your left hand or your right hand, well, it's the same with pigeons. Though your champion pigeon has no weak sides and is totally balanced. But with lesser pigeons, one wing works harder than the other. All pigeons have it. You must breed it out of the pigeon. How do you see it? Anyone can see it but people just don't see it as a fault. So I look at the bone structure and

282

the wings, and I look at the throat of the pigeon, which shows if it's had a lot of disease before in its life. I look at its lung capacity and, lastly, I look at the eye. And even if everything seems fine up to then, I might find a mistake in the eye. But if I find a weak vent bone I won't go any further. I've handled so many pigeons, I just know.'

If Joe knew so much maybe he could answer a question that had been lurking in my mind since day one. I'd asked it before but never got a straight and fathomable answer, so I thought I'd try it on the pigeon masters of the southern hemisphere. Why did people from Albania to Azerbaijan love the feathered miracle? What was it about the pigeon that got people so worked up and obsessed?

'I don't know whether it's a love of nature or a love of animals. I can't really explain it,' said Joe. Not even he knew.

'Are you asking why?' Ron suddenly chipped in. 'Why?' he repeated.

'Yes, why?' I said.

'Why pigeons? In one word — passion. The passion is something you cannot take out of the pigeon fancier,' Ron said before clenching his jaw a little and staring out rather wistfully over the many drinkers in the Rhino bar.

'It's inside you,' added Laurence, 'it's just

something inside you.'

'It's like this,' continued Ron, leaning forward and looking as serious as you could after a good few drinks. 'The personality of the person within the pigeon fancier is striving to achieve something with the pigeon that may be beyond what he can achieve without it.'

'Like flying?'

'More than that.'

I was more flummoxed than I'd ever been in my entire life. I don't think the beer was helping any of us (especially Ron).

'The fact that you can't understand the thing means that it is very difficult to explain to the non pigeon fancier,' said Ron. 'And I don't think that anyone can explain it fully. What drives a pigeon fancier to be a pigeon fancier? What I think and believe is there seems to be a drive within that person that drives him to success. Whether that be the working-class bloke from England or an average Kiwi bloke who wants to buy pigeons on a Saturday or whatever, or he's an injured sportsman who can't play rugby any more or can't play soccer, and all of a sudden he's got this interest. Why? It's the adrenaline rush of winning, like if you win bingo or go and win money on a horse race, and like those people who gamble on slot machines. Why do they play slot machines? It's not just the pigeon, it's the person. It's the competitive nature within yourself. Some people like goldfish and you can sit there and watch it and it lowers your heart rate.'

So it's the competition, the winning and the passion. Now we were getting somewhere. Was that it, then, in Ron's expert opinion? Did that put a lid on it?

'You can't really say. No one can really say for sure,' he concluded with an enigmatic shrug.

Perhaps it was beyond me. Ron certainly thought so. He was a pigeon man after all, and it was beyond him. Maybe I'd find out before I left Africa, or at least before I felt the cold blade of the Reaper's scythe.

'We are here to win the race,' said Laurence, 'that is all that matters.'

'OK, so who's going to win the race?'

'Impossible to answer that question,' Ron replied.

'Who's been the most consistent, then, over the years?'

'I'll answer your question,' said Laurence. Laurence said that he'd been pretty consistent and that he had a good chance and didn't fear anyone. Not the Germans, the Belgians or the 'Poms'.

'Zandy, the organizer of this pigeon race,

said in front of many people, 'This is the most constant pigeon fancier in South Africa. Anywhere you want to go, his name is there. He pays his money and he fuckin' beats 'em and if he doesn't beat 'em he's in the mix.' In the South African race this year I won the race by two hours and I was second as well. The rest came in on Sunday. You can't argue with the facts.'

By this point I reckoned Ron could argue with the patron saint of facts, albeit with a smile on his face. 'I don't think you can answer that question,' he retorted. 'You cannot say who is the best over the ten years because statistically, if you were a professor and you wanted to get down to the nuts and bolts of it, you'd have to get down to the chromosomes and the genetics and the anatomy of all this, break it all down and split the atom. What you have to look at is how many birds he has in the race.' Ron pointed at Colin. 'Germany could have 500. Australia could have 300. New Zealand could have twenty. If you put it into the perspective of what the entries were and what the results are, then what you have is an overview and then you look at it on a percentage basis to see who has done best. It may not necessarily be the Germans or the Belgians.' That was as clear as pigeon shit. But Ron looked like he knew what he was trying to say, even if I didn't.

'So there isn't a man or a woman you can pick out and say they have been the most consistent?'

'No one can say,' said Ron. 'No one can say who has been the best in this race because of the reasons I've just given you.'

It was hopeless and I was getting nowhere. As I sat back and Ron had another gulp of his drink to lubricate the larynx, and the night and the beer swept their dark cloaks over us all, I turned to see the answer to my question walk into the bar.

In amongst a crowd of short-sleeved, bespectacled men was one of the most famous, bespectacled pigeon racing men of them all. Gerard Koopman. The Abramovich of pigeon racing had arrived and he was ordering a round of beers just behind our table. If Koopman was here what chance did any of us have?

I stumbled over to his table (it was getting late).

'Didn't think it was your kind of race. Les didn't want to bother,' I slurred to Gerard.

'I like to come here and do a little gambling and I like the race more now,' said Gerard grinning confidently. 'This is the new goal in my life, to win the biggest race. Or try to win so when you win it you have won it.'

'Koopman. Now he's a pigeon racer,' said Ron on my return, although Joe wasn't so sure if the great man would figure in the top places. 'If there is one thing that is sure about this race, it's that the bird that wins probably hasn't even figured yet,' said Joe. 'Probably hasn't even shown its true colours.' The men at the table nodded. 'It's up there now and all we know is it has what it takes to win.'

'And what's that?'

'Genetics, good breeding and consistency.'

'And stamina?' I asked.

'Of course. Because it's a long race. There's a lot to deal with.'

It was a marathon. I knew that much.

18

That's Pigeons

I could fly higher than an eagle,
For you are the wind beneath my wings

Larry Henley,
'Wind Beneath My Wings'

The loud banging and shouting at the hotel door came at eight a.m. I thought it was a police raid, the banging was that loud, but then I remembered I hadn't done anything wrong the night before and that it was just Laurence and Joe. Laurence barged in moaning that he hadn't slept, followed by a smiling Joe, carrying a four-pack of beer.

'Get up, you lazy Pommie bastard. Today's the big day. The pigeons are flying!' Laurence said as he thrust a beer in my hand.

Laurence was excited, very excited, and so was Joe. They'd been waiting for this race all year, as had I, but these two were crazy when it came to pigeons. The way they were acting in the few hours before the pigeons came back to the loft, you would have thought they were five-year-old children on Christmas Eve — it was all thrilling, but they were gripped with a fear that Santa might not show up.

'Let's ring Uncle Wal,' said Laurence grabbing the phone. 'Shall we ring Uncle Wal?'

'Who is Uncle Wal?' I enquired.

'Uncle Wal is a genius,' said Laurence. 'That guy knows what pigeons are about, he can tell you everything you want to know about them. Let's ring Uncle Wal.'

They rang Uncle Wal. I got washed and dressed, and when I re-entered the room I could hear Uncle Wal's slow South African drawl droning loudly out of the telephone intercom. 'Is he his real Uncle?' I asked Joe quietly. He just shrugged.

Uncle Wal was seventy-five and he was an amateur meteorologist and a whizzo pigeon fancier according to Laurence. 'What is the wind going to be like, Uncle Wal?' Laurence asked.

'I'll go and check the weather vane,' Uncle Wal replied.

We all had another drink, then Laurence ordered some more. Suddenly it seemed like the night before had never ended. It hadn't in Laurence's mind. Uncle Wal returned after what seemed like a very long time.

'That weather vane of mine is only six

knots.' I think that was what Uncle Wal said, although it was loud and fuzzy, and it sounded like he was outside in a strong wind.

Laurence was concentrating hard on the intercom and hanging on Uncle Wal's every word.

'What else, Uncle Wal, what else?' said Laurence impatiently.

'The wind will push them towards Pretoria. It will be sitting rrrright on their noses,' said Uncle Wal, rolling the 'r'.

'If you see my pigeons, send them my regards, Uncle Wal,' said Laurence, and then the call was over and Uncle Wal was gone.

'Did you hear that? Did you hear what Uncle Wal said?' his face red with excitement.

'Yes,' I said. 'What does it all mean?'

'It means it's going to be a hard fuckin' race today, boy. Fuck me, its going to be a hard race today.'

Laurence and Joe left after several more beers and lots more pigeon chat, and already drained, I walked down to the Superbowl to get a good seat for the big race. The pigeons had been liberated from a place called Trompsberg and, according to Laurence and Uncle Wal, the first pigeon would be due back at around two-thirty p.m., give or take half an hour.

The Superbowl was already buzzing with

tense and excited pigeon fanciers at midday. There were 1,667 international entries and 735 from South Africa. There were 217 from the United Kingdom and 36 from Ireland, with 31 countries represented in all, from Belgium to Belarus and from Slovenia to Saudi Arabia. Many of them had sent representatives to the Superbowl and were milling around, chatting, eating and drinking, and a flag for each country was draped over the balcony which stretched around the auditorium.

Paul was there, scrubbed and grinning. 'When do you expect them back, Paul?' I asked.

'If I had a pound for everyone who's asked me that this morning,' he said smiling. It was the question on the edge of everyone's lips. Paul said the same as Laurence and Uncle Wal: the first would probably be back around two-thirty although the strong headwind didn't favour a quick race.

We still had thirty pigeons in the race as there were no casualties after the birds were sent. So the Jimmy Richards-bred pigeons, who'd survived and were liberated at Trompsberg on the day of the race, in no particular order, were as follows:

Wonderman, Wondergirl, Superman, Lightning, Hurricane, Express, Prospector, Something Special, Something Gold,

Luckycharm, Natalie, Sundancer, Sund-owner, Sun City, Pot of Gold and Heartbreaker.

The thirteen additional pigeons Paul had purchased on the net with the money left over from the syndicate were:

Syndale Horse, Syndale Dog, Fontwell Chance, Kulic, Marius, Olive Branch, Kleine Zensi, Million Dollar Baby, Fly Away, Dream Racer, Dewey, My Lover and the bizarrely named misogynistic pigeon, Chauvinist.

Entertainment was laid on to calm the nerves of all the pigeon people in the Superbowl prior to the big moment. An attractive female singer was belting out a few standards, with organ accompaniment, on the stage in front of the VIP tables. I was one of the VIPs — that tells you the standard of the VIP.

'One Moment in Time', 'I Need a Hero' . . . the girl sang and nobody clapped. Then she was replaced with an opera singer, who sang 'Nessun Dorma' among others. Nobody clapped her much either. Maybe everyone was too tense. That's what Ron said when I bumped into him. Ron and Colin and a few of their mates and their wives and girlfriends were in the Superbowl wearing New Zealand team colours: black with a large silver fern.

'The tension is too much for some people,' said Ron. 'Some people handle it differently from others.'

'How do you handle it?'

'I just get drunk,' Ron said laughing.

I felt like getting drunk too but I restrained myself. I would hold off until I had something to celebrate.

It was tough, though, staying sober in that environment. It was as though I was in a room with several thousand expectant fathers, clammy palms and sweaty faces all around. People shuffled through the auditorium, mainly middle-aged men in short-sleeved plaid shirts, with faces like refugees in a nuclear bunker waiting for the white noise. I'd seen it with Les in the Portland combine. Tense, nervous, irritable. They didn't look like they were enjoying it.

'It gets to you,' said Ron. 'It's a part of you flying out there. It's a part of you feeling the heat and the wind.'

I was feeling the wind but that was probably the early morning beers. Occasionally these pained pigeon men would glance up at one of the two big screens that had been erected to show the climax of the race, but there was nothing to see yet. The screens showed only the tedious Google Earth slo-mo virtual route of the pigeon race.

As well as the unappreciated music, a buffet had been laid on for the VIPs. Everyone else had to pay. A large queue of Important People holding plates were lifting up silver pots filled with hot dogs and beef burgers and various types of spud. I saw Abramovich/Koopman in front of one of the silver pots, shovelling chips onto his plate and then struggling to squeeze a dollop of tomato sauce onto his burger bun. He shook the bottle and stared into the eye of it, but the sauce was having none of it, so after a while he gave in. Was it an omen? Were our pigeons going to be stubborn and not bother turning up, like the last dregs of ketchup in a sauce bottle? It was possible. Even Koopman looked human, and not his usual *über* pigeon-man self, as he glumly walked back to the table filled with Dutch fanciers with sauceless chips and burger in hand.

As in Blackpool, those in the pigeon product-selling industry were out in force, and stands selling the usual goods had been erected all over the hall. For want of anything else to do I gawped at a few: vitamins, laxatives, rat scarers. Unikon Electronic Timing System — who had supplied the ETS for the race — had a stand, while others were selling worm remedies and blood purifiers. After the night I'd had with Laurence and Ron I was tempted to buy some of that. There was also a stand promoting the Europa pigeon race in Cardiff.

I asked the small man with the grey hair near the stand where all the British pigeon men were. 'Probably pissed or having a fag. Who knows?' said the man.

He was called Tony Cowan and he was from Cardiff. Tony said he was something of a movie star in pigeon racing. 'Do you know I'm the most famous man in China?' he said shaking my hand. He told me he had been the managing director of the biggest pigeon publishing company in the world. He had written books, made videos and appeared on radio and TV all over the world, including China. 'Yes, I'm the most famous man in China,' he told me again.

'How so?'

'I've been flying the flag for the sport all around the world. Working in the business for over thirty years and I still know fuck all about pigeons. Don't think anybody does to be honest with you. There's more black magic and voodoo in this game than any other sport in existence. Load of bloody bollocks it is.'

Tony was doing a good job of talking up

pigeons. I liked his style. He had the fast and mumbling delivery of the 1970s off-pier comic, his hair was slightly bouffed and his shirt had one too many buttons open.

'Anyway, about fifteen years ago this wealthy Chinaman came to my office in London.' He paused and looked over his shoulder to wait for a reaction from the audience, which was me. 'And he said, 'Tony, I want to buy your videos.' I said, 'When are you going to buy them?' He said, 'If you give me a copy I'll take them back and send you an order.' So I gave him one copy of fifteen different titles.

'He took the lot and I sat back expecting a mega, mega order and it never came. He copied them of course, didn't he. So consequently we got sweet FA, but they tell me every pub and club in China has my ugly face up there, which is something, I suppose.'

As well as being the most famous man in China, Tony knew Les Green. In fact Tony told me he had taught Les everything he knew, at least in terms of Les's dynamic auctioneering technique.

'That's what I do now, you see, I auction pigeons. Les rang me and asked me how he should face an audience. I said, 'I don't believe you can sell anything with a long face.' I said to him, 'For Christ's sake, wind 'em up'.

'I did auctions in the East End of London, and I used to take the piss out of punters. You used to get all kinds in there: gangsters, boxers, all types. I used to call them poofs. That's the way I am, I can't be serious. It goes back to a book I read a number of years ago by a Greek millionaire. He had no money and he borrowed his mate's best car, and went and bought himself a sun lamp, and he went around selling investments. His philosophy was: if you go round and knock on somebody's door with a push bike and a face as white as a skull, you'll sell fuck all. But if you go round with a nice smile, bronzed and in a nice suit and driving a nice car that doesn't belong to you, you'll do all right. It's the image factor, you see, it's important, and that's how I've always carried on.'

'What about the image factor of pigeon racing? How does that stand up? Is it bronzed with gleaming teeth and a nice car, or is it on a push bike and white as a skull?' I asked.

'That's a good question. A very good question. That's what needs to improve — the image factor of pigeon racing is totally wrong. Flat caps and brown ale and all that. I deal with kings, queens, princes all the way down. My best client, one of them anyway, is a billionaire. I've dealt with all kinds; they come in all shapes and sizes. Some are millionaires and some are as scruffy as arseholes. The image has to change if we are to get anywhere.'

One man who was brought to South Africa to help improve the image of pigeon racing was Carlo Napolitano, the Queen's pigeon loft manager. He managed the 160 or so pigeons at the Queen's loft in Sandringham, and Paul — to help with the PR for the race — had persuaded him to enter six of the Queen's pigeons into the race.

Carlo joined Tony and me at the stand. He looked like Murray Walker: he was bald with silver-rimmed spectacles, and he looked a little bit miserable.

'Is the Queen looking forward to the race?' I asked him.

'Well, I wouldn't say she's looking forward to it, but she knows she's got some pigeons competing,' he said in a slow, deliberate, Norfolk accent.

Carlo had sent six of the Queen's finest to the loft in Sun City but that number had been reduced to four before the race day, which, compared with the irate Mexican, was a fairly good ratio. The Queen's pigeons were pretty good pigeons, though, and Carlo had been a racer himself for many years in King's

Lynn and was a decent pigeon man.

'Is she a fan of the pigeon then, the Queen?' I asked.

'Her Majesty likes pigeons, yes,' said Carlo. 'But the first pigeon person in the family was George V. He had them when he was the Prince of Wales and then George VI, the Queen's father, also kept them, and then it went on like that. It's tradition. Whether the next king or queen will carry it on remains to be seen,' he finished somewhat mournfully.

'It'd be nice to see William and Kate Middleton here,' I said. Carlo nodded. I had a picture in my head of them half-cut and cheering their pigeons home in the Rhino bar. I'm sure $200,000 wouldn't go amiss, although Carlo was at pains to stress that the Queen got no financial gain from entering the race. Any money handbagged by HM would go into her charity pot.

'Have you ever met her?' I asked, before Carlo sauntered off.

'Oh yes. I meet her around once or twice a year. She's very down-to-earth. She's very relaxed at Sandringham. Although she hasn't been round this year. I last saw her when I got called up to get a Christmas box.'

'What did you get?'

'A very stylish silver picture frame,' said Carlo. Lovely stuff.

By two o'clock the electric charges of excitement were tangible in the Superbowl. So much so the opera singer's microphone broke and the acoustics went all wonky, much to the distress of some and the relief of others. Outside the Superbowl a large crowd was standing in a fog of smoke as they nervously chuffed on cigarettes in the designated smoking area.

The screens changed from Google Earth to images of a man standing in a watchtower above the loft in Sun City. Laurence and Joe were sat up in the balcony with a bunch of South Africans garbed in patriotic dress — brightly patterned shirts à la Nelson Mandela, and South African rugby tops — and drinking and staring at the two screens for any sign of a pigeon on the horizon.

I plonked myself down at the table with a limp Union Jack stuck in the centre of it. A couple of pigeon racers from Dorset were seated there, as well as an old man with small teeth who was drinking a can of Fanta.

I thought it only appropriate to join my fellow countrymen to see our boys, hopefully triumphant, return to the loft. So I pulled up a chair between the old man and a big, ruddy-cheeked bloke with a bald head and a grey moustache. The bald man told me his name was Robbie. Robbie had a broad West Country accent. The old man was called Guy. 'Guy's got an OBE,' said Robbie after a minute or two. Guy smiled and drank his Fanta. I didn't ask what for and he didn't tell me — I presumed services to pigeons.

Robbie told me he was a businessman and a pigeon racer from Plymouth. He had won a British National in 2005 and one of his pigeons had finished sixth in the Million Dollar race in 2000 — $21,000 in his sky rocket for that triumph.

'What time do you think the birds will be back?' I asked Robbie. He just shrugged.

'Three-thirty, I reckon,' said a man sat across from Robbie and me who appeared to have every inch of his body tattooed, apart from his head which was just pierced in various places. To alleviate the tedium the pigeon men on the table had started a sweepstake: twenty rand a go to guess the time the first pigeon came in. I joined in to pass the time. 2.45 was my guess.

As the clock moved to three, still no pigeons. I looked around the auditorium and saw Ron and the New Zealand team on a table not far away. Ron smiled and raised his beer. I waved back.

A few of the racers on the UK table didn't look very happy, especially the man with the tattoos. 'Is it the nerves?' I asked Robbie.

'Yeah, this is the horrible part, the waiting,' he said. 'And we just had a phone call from home.'

'Bad news?'

'Yes,' said Robbie looking very serious.

Had the Americans bombed Iran? Had the North Koreans invaded the Isle of Wight?

'There's been a bird flu outbreak at the Bernard Matthews turkey farm. Could be bad for racing next year.'

I didn't know what to say. What can you say when you hear something like that?

'The pigeons shouldn't be long now,' said Robbie, the grimace turning to a smile. I hoped not; the suspense was killing me and I was in desperate need of the khazi. Surely I could wait, I thought. I wasn't a five-year-old. 'Do you think I'll get back in time if I go?' I said to Robbie.

He looked at his watch. 'Should be fine,' he said. 'No sign of 'em yet.' There was a strong wind on the pigeons' noses after all, according to Uncle Wal.

I left the auditorium. But it wasn't fine. It was far from fine.

I heard the eruption and the wild cheers as I was approaching the urinal. I raced back, fighting my way past a herd of rotund pigeon men to see the third- and fourth-placed pigeons on-screen hanging around outside the loft. The pigeons had to walk into the trap to register in the placings.

The first pigeons were already in. I'd missed them, that much was obvious from the cheers and the jubilation all around. A year of my life and several thousand miles and continents and I'd missed the climax. But there was no time for moping. Had we won and, if not, who had? Who'd bagged the big one?

I fought my way back and saw a group of men not far from our table laughing and hugging for a moment. I thought Paul was one of them.

It looked promising. The optimism and the dream lasted a minute, however, maybe less. As I reached the table I saw that it wasn't Paul, just some grey-haired man in a blue shirt. There were plenty of them around. I looked at Robbie and then at the tattooed man. Their faces were as long as the queue for the toilets.

'Who won the race?' I asked, now conceding the fact that it probably wasn't me and definitely wasn't one of them.

'The Germans,' said the tattooed man before taking a long mournful drink of his beer. 'The fuckin' Krauts,' he said, less than magnanimously.

Robbie was more forgiving and filled me in on what had happened. Two birds had appeared, like Omar Sharif at the beginning of *Lawrence of Arabia*, at seven minutes past three, about a minute after I'd gone to the loo. They had circled and landed on the loft and one had hung around for a bit — I bet his owner was happy — and the other went into the trap and was recorded on the ETS system at seven minutes past three and thirteen seconds. The pigeon was called Konstantin and it was owned by Helmut and Alfons Klaas from Germany.

The second pigeon — Schalke — was also German and a pigeon named Doctor Feelgood, also German, plopped in to take the third spot — I did see that. I saw the third pigeon walk in as Robbie filled me in on the tale of the winning birds, so the trip wasn't a total waste.

People cheered and more pigeons appeared. Prizes were given to the first 250 home, which were coming in five and ten minutes apart, sometimes two or three at a time, appearing as dots in the clear blue sky. They came, little wings flapping like the clappers, and then they circled and landed on the loft, hung around and eventually walked into the trap, people cheering and laughing. That's what happened. Pigeon racing wasn't the greatest spectator sport, the highlight being the walk into the loft. But people enjoyed it — lots of people. All around me Germans were hugging and kissing each other.

The tattooed man didn't seem to be enjoying it that much though. 'All the best birds in Germany are from ours,' he told us all. 'The ones that were left there during the war. Our pigeons went over there and they commandeered them.' I didn't know whether he was joking, but he didn't look like he was. He sat impassive and took a large gulp of his drink.

I doubted the tattooed man was correct, however. I doubted the German pigeons were ours. I think he was making it up, clinging on to a wispy thread of hope that we were somehow connected to the winning pigeons.

We all sat around and waited to see if we had picked up any of the minor placings. We hadn't. The Germans had cleared the board: sixteen of the top twenty birds were all German. I wondered why they were so good.

'They are good pigeon racers, the Germans,' said Robbie. You could say that again. Nobody seemed to know for sure why the Germans had done so well and we hadn't. It was a mystery. Robbie just shrugged and then said cheerily, 'Let's have another go next year.' Robbie had taken it well and so had all the others on the table except the tattooed man, who was still talking about the war. 'At least we won the war,' he said. Yes, we hadn't won the pigeon race but we'd been a part of the Allied Forces that emerged victorious in the Second World War over sixty years ago. There was always that to console ourselves with.

The highest British placing was twenty-eighth with a pigeon owned by Paul McCarthy — the man who had won the Honda Civic in the Hot Spot — called Wallasey Lass.

I hung around and watched the first forty pigeons fly back to the loft and then I left. There was no sign of a Paul Smith syndicate pigeon anywhere and I'd had enough excitement for one day.

The next day I took a stroll down to the pigeon auction in the Superbowl to see if any of ours had made it back before dark, or at all. The winning pigeons were being sold off to various pigeon men, mostly Chinese, and the winning bird was sold to a South African for $38,000. Paul was smiling again. He looked happy.

'Well, we didn't win but we didn't do bad at all,' he said.

'No?'

'211th,' he said.

'Oh, that's not bad at all,' I replied.

'We haven't won much but at least we were up there. And we had the last one in of the

307

day: 255th. It arrived at five to eleven. One of Jimmy Richards' pigeons, Something Special.' Paul was happy with that, and I was happy for Jimmy.

'Why did the Germans do so well?'

Paul didn't know for sure. 'They were just very good pigeons. It happens like that sometimes and when it does you've just got to tip your hat and say well done . . . if you know what I mean.'

Paul asked me if I'd enjoyed the pigeon experience and if I was coming back next year for another crack. I told him that I'd enjoyed it very much, but that I probably wouldn't be coming back. I'd had my share of pigeon excitement for one lifetime. I'd done my stint in the loft, in the pub and in Blackpool. It was time for me to bow out with what remained of my sanity intact. Paul shook my hand and walked towards a bunch of very happy-looking men who'd just bought one of the pigeons for $15,000.

I walked out of the auditorium and strolled back to the Palace of the Lost City. I was still tired from the journey and needed some rest. On the way I bumped into Joe, who was buying drinks at the Rhino bar. He called me over to say goodbye.

'Did you have any luck in the race?' I asked.

'No,' said Joe. 'It's the first time I haven't finished in the top 200. I can't understand it.' He rubbed his head but didn't look too concerned, though. He was smiling. Joe was philosophical and I knew he would be back. He did, after all, have a feather up his arse. 'I don't know what happened. The Germans had a great race, what can you say? That happens sometimes. You can sit around trying to figure things out or you can get on with selecting pigeons that can get you into the top positions next year. There's no point in getting too down about these things.'

I told him he was right. I shook his hand and wished him luck with his pigeons and everything else.

'Sometimes you win and sometimes you don't,' said Joe raising his beer. 'That's pigeons.'

Epilogue

Back to Our Roots

The cheque for my winnings from the Paul Smith syndicate arrived several weeks after I returned from South Africa.

'I'm afraid you only won £5.78,' read the note under the cheque for that amount, 'and I ask you to pay this into your bank account as soon as possible.' That didn't sound good. Surely Paul didn't do that badly out of the deal that he was worried about a five quid cheque bouncing?

Five pounds and seventy-eight pence. Not quite the $200,000 I'd been aiming for, but it would stretch to a packet of fags and possibly a bag of Wotsits.

'Put the money on a horse,' Frank suggested as I stared at the feeble fruits of my labour. Frank was very amused by the Sun City result but a nag was a fairly adequate suggestion. Find a six to one shot, get a forty pound win and then stick it on the next horse. Maybe I would soon be on a roll. Or maybe not.

My time in pigeons was over, I knew that much. If I never saw a pigeon again I didn't think I'd be too concerned. I had one final duty, though: to see Les and wish him luck as the 2007 season approached. And it sounded like they were in need of some. The spectre of bird flu still hovered like one of Ken Livingstone's Harris hawks ready to savage the pigeon racing season at the drop of a dead bird, and I'd heard there were serious changes afoot at the Wall, Lunt, Galley and Green headquarters in Oldham.

Paul Galley was no longer part of the team and Les and the gang had been forced to move from the Oldham Federation, and in turn the warehouse loft. Once again they'd been victims of their own success and were on their way back to Irlam, and the Warrington Federation, to start from scratch.

'That fuckin' dog has gone,' Les explained. And the cabin was empty apart from a few pigeon supplies and Pat's frying pan. 'We've sold all the old pigeons,' he said as he removed the last of the pigeon boxes from the windswept roof. 'We're just training young-sters now. Nobody wants us to race round here. They're jumpin' off roofs to get away from us,' he said sounding surprisingly upbeat despite the drawback.

'We were too good for 'em basically. The

Oldham Fed didn't like their noses being rubbed in the shit and they're having silly meetings in their kitchens, having words with each other to work out the best way to get rid of us. We all knew this had been going on since the middle of last year so we knew what was coming.'

The Oldham Federation had basically had enough of Les and the boys. Their opponents, as had happened before, had got sick of playing catch-up and tired of Les's burly shadow hanging over all things pigeon-related. Les and his team were professionals in a sport played by amateurs. So a pigeon coup had taken place. The lesser pigeon man had risen up and ousted Les and the boys and their squadron of ace pigeons from the Oldham landscape. So Les was left with no choice: he was going back to his roots. Back to Irlam, where all the success had begun over a decade ago.

'To be honest, it suits us because we've been away from Warrington for the past few years and they've all come back,' said Les. 'Those who thought we had gone came back so it's got bigger and bigger. Now it's a great opportunity to go back there. It makes life a lot easier for us and the competition is good again, so we can be racing against between five and eight thousand pigeons a week. It'll be good while it lasts, but we'll have to wait and see how long it does. That lot at Warrington don't like us either,' he added, laughing.

'But we never resigned so they have to let us back in, they've got no choice. We've heard the rumblings already though: 'Oh fuck, they're not back already, are they?''

Despite the enforced move, Les was still looking to the future, as well as what lay ahead in the Warrington Fed. He still had ideas; big plans to take pigeon racing and himself, his birds and his partners into another league entirely. And a bit further than Skelmersdale, too. The Orient was in his sights — the Far East, not Leyton. Les had plans to take his pigeons to the salivating jaws of the Red Dragon.

'We are into China now,' said Les excitedly. 'We are trying to get into Beijing at the minute, advertising in the Chinese magazines, and the Philippines and Portugal. It's fuckin' huge over there!'

There was no time to sit moping in the coop, Les reckoned. A window of great opportunity was opening in China and Les had his crowbar and rope ladder at the ready.

'There's 650,000 fanciers registered in China and they reckon there's at least as many not registered. You know what it's like over there for gambling, they go fuckin' crazy for it. They are not really arsed about being members of unions — they will have their own races and race for $50,000 a time,' he said, shifting some old papers and sitting down on the bench in the empty cabin.

'I'm doing a sale for a kid in Belgium, and this lad is probably the biggest importer of pigeons into China in the world. A guy called Emile Denis. And Emile promised me that he would open doors for me in China 'cause I'm opening doors for him. I'm introducing his pigeons into Britain.'

China was the new frontier for pigeon men on the lookout to conquer new territories and make a few quid. There was feathered gold in them thar hills. But there were a few problems. There was gold in the Chinese hills, but there were also bandits. It wasn't going to be an easy ride into town for Les and his pals from Holland and Belgium.

'Koopman won't have any more auctions there. He says it's very difficult to get your money once you have sold 'em. The fuckers want 30 per cent of the sale, plus 20 per cent of the advertising, so you're 50 per cent down, and the mafia get involved and you've got to pay 'em protection money or they don't let people turn up at the auctions.'

Les said it 'sounded far fetched'. But the

Chinese mafia had a habit of standing on the door of the pigeon sales and barring anyone from entering if they hadn't received a cut of the feathered booty.

'You've got to give them 10 per cent so you're only getting 40 per cent of the sale, and when you think that it costs you 130 euro per pigeon to get 'em there, you've got to make really big money to get anything out of it. So does it make sense to go over there when the end result might mean you only get a hundred quid per pigeon? I think it's like this: you've got to swallow a bit of shit, haven't yer? You've got to give 'em the pigeons for nothing, basically, introduce your pigeons to China and once they start winning, they are going to want them and then you're in the driving seat. You've got to establish yourself, then once you've got a foothold in the market and your birds start winning dough over there, they'll all want 'em. Then you're the one wearing the pants. So that is our aim. We are going to have to get our pigeons out there. I'm going to take Emile Denis up on his offer, basically knowing I'm going to get shafted, but looking at the bigger picture. No good being small-minded, is there? We are going to have to eat a bit of shit. You've got to be in it to win it. It's as simple as that.'

I was going to frame the cheque but I decided to take Frank's advice and put it on a horse. What did I have to lose? Five pounds thirty-eight. I scoured the *Racing Post* and found the perfect nag: Investment Wings it was called. Running in the three-thirty from Catterick. 'Stands a great chance,' said the *Racing Post*. I put the money on, stood back and waited. It came in seventh.